# SPSS FOR RESEARCH METHODS

## A Basic Guide

**Georjeanna Wilson-Doenges**
University of Wisconsin—Green Bay

W. W. Norton & Company, Inc.
New York • London

W. W. Norton & Company has been independent since its founding in 1923, when William Warder Norton and Mary D. Herter Norton first published lectures delivered at the People's Institute, the adult education division of New York City's Cooper Union. The firm soon expanded its program beyond the Institute, publishing books by celebrated academics from America and abroad. By midcentury, the two major pillars of Norton's publishing program—trade books and college texts—were firmly established. In the 1950s, the Norton family transferred control of the company to its employees, and today—with a staff of four hundred and a comparable number of trade, college, and professional titles published each year—W. W. Norton & Company stands as the largest and oldest publishing house owned wholly by its employees.

Courtesy of International Business Machines Corporation, © International Business Machines Corporation. "SPSS Inc." was acquired by IBM in October, 2009. IBM SPSS Statistics software ("SPSS"). IBM, the IBM logo, ibm.com, and SPSS are trademarks or registered trademarks of International Business Machines Corporation, registered in many jurisdictions worldwide. Other product and service names might be trademarks of IBM or other companies. A current list of IBM trademarks is available on the Web at "IBM Copyright and trademark information" at www.ibm.com/legal/copytrade.shtml.

Editor: Sheri Snavely
Editorial Assistant: Scott Sugarman
Project Editor: Sujin Hong
Production Manager: Eric Pier-Hocking
Marketing Manager, Psychology: Lauren Winkler
Design Director: Hope Miller Goodell
Photo Editor: Stephanie Romeo
Composition: Cenveo® Publisher Services
Illustrations Studio: Cenveo Publisher Services
Manufacturing: LSC Communications, Kendallville

**ISBN: 978-0-393-93882-1 (pbk.)**

W. W. Norton & Company , Inc., 500 Fifth Avenue, New York, NY 10110

wwnorton.com

W. W. Norton & Company Ltd., 15 Carlisle Street, London W1D 3BS

5 6 7 8 9 0

For my father, my inspiration

For my father, my inspiration

# About the Author

**Georjeanna Wilson-Doenges** is Associate Professor of Psychology at the University of Wisconsin, Green Bay. She received her Ph.D. from the University of California, Irvine. Her research interests involve individuals' interpretation of sense of community, student engagement in college, experiential learning, and assessment of undergraduate psychology learning outcomes. She has taught research methods and statistics courses with an SPSS lab component for over 20 years. Year after year, she has refined her teaching to help students who are often fearful of data analysis by making her courses engaging, and to promote success in even the most math-insecure students. Throughout her career, Dr. Wilson-Doenges has emphasized teaching and writing about data analysis in clear and accessible ways.

# Brief Contents

# Preface

Data analysis plays a crucial role in the science of psychology. The most innovative research can be flawed by improper handling of data, while the skillful reading of results can shed new light in surprising places. To succeed in statistics and research methods courses—and to prepare themselves for whatever research they take on—students must develop strong data analysis skills. As SPSS is one of the most commonly used software packages for data analysis in the social sciences, I wrote this guide to help students with little or no experience to quickly and independently familiarize themselves with the program basics.

Instructors often say that they prefer to focus their lectures on the content of statistics and research methods without getting bogged down in the computer skills required for data analysis. Over 20 years of teaching these courses, I have seen that covering the essentials of SPSS takes up valuable class time that would often be better spent illustrating key concepts with real-world, research-based examples. In addition, students most effectively learn the operation of SPSS by using it, hands-on, but it is difficult to teach one-on-one when there are usually at least 25 students per class.

This guide fosters SPSS skill development outside the classroom. It is easy to read and enables students to build their knowledge of the software at their own pace. The examples in each chapter walk students through all the aspects of data analysis by including the research question, a brief description of the method, the data entered, the SPSS commands relevant to the research question, the SPSS output, an interpretation of the output, and the corresponding results section written in APA style. Each step is clearly indicated by a banner in the margins, and screen shots ensure that the instructions in the text are as clear as possible. I believe that instructors will have the freedom to spend more of their class time presenting engaging content, knowing that their students have this guide to help them along the way.

Another major challenge to teaching data analysis is that students are often anxious about learning statistics and using SPSS. This guide aims to dispel those fears. Jargon-heavy, dense paragraphs, and abstract presentations of concepts can leave students feeling more than a little confused, so I consistently stayed with succinct, step-by-step explanations. The examples, which stem from topics my own students have been excited to test, like the relations between having a tattoo and perceived intelligence or hours spent playing video games and GPA, should feel familiar and compelling. The screen shots are overlaid with arrows that point to the functions necessary for each step of data analysis. Thanks to these features, students will learn to efficiently complete rigorous statistical analyses.

Should students decide to hold on to this guide beyond their statistics and research methods courses, they will also see that it is an ideal reference text. Whether they have recently used SPSS or if they just need to remind themselves of how a function works, the book's streamlined structure, clear writing style, and numerous screen shots make for a great quick refresher.

By the time they have finished reading this guide, I hope that students will feel confident about using SPSS—and that their instructors will have seen the results. If our students can develop strong data analysis skills, they will be well equipped to make significant contributions to psychology and other research-oriented fields.

## Acknowledgments

Writing an SPSS guide was never something I even considered until my esteemed colleague and friend, Regan Gurung, suggested it. I am forever grateful for his encouragement and prodding, without which I would never have begun this process. As a first-time author, I could not have asked for a more wonderful editorial team than Sheri Snavely and Scott Sugarman. They provided the most reassuring and encouraging writing environment. Their constant positivity and support made working on this guide a pleasure. The inspiration for this guide came from Beth Morling's superb *Research Methods in Psychology* text. Her approach of critically examining research makes so much sense to my students, and her wonderful examples make psychological research come alive for them. I am also so thankful for the fabulous reviewers who made the book so much better through their careful and detailed revisions:

Jennifer Asmuth, *Susquehanna University*

Rachel Dinero, *Cazenovia College*

Regan Gurung, *University of Wisconsin—Green Bay*

Beth Morling, *University of Delaware*

I am blessed every day to be surrounded by the best colleagues in the world at the University of Wisconsin—Green Bay. They inspire me and have been amazing examples of what it truly means to be teachers and scholars. Last, but certainly not least, I could not have accomplished this project without the love and support of my family. My father, who passed away in the midst of writing this guide, was always my biggest fan, and I am grateful for his lifelong support of my dreams and accomplishments. My kids, Jordan and Julia, and my husband, Vern, are my amazing cheerleaders. I love how they support me both personally and professionally. My family also made sure that I didn't work too much—because life is too short to miss out on the small and great moments you take for granted.

# Contents

## CORRELATIONAL RESEARCH: TESTING ASSOCIATION CLAIMS

# EXPERIMENTAL RESEARCH: MAKING CAUSAL CLAIMS

*Regression analyses provide students with a glimpse into how science begins to explain behavior by demonstrating how different variables can be used to predict outcomes. Multivariate Regression allows us to statistically control for third variables to increase validity in correlational studies. In this chapter we walk students through multivariate correlational analyses including testing for moderation and mediation.*

*Comparing sample means is one of the most common statistical procedures to test for significance of a simple experimental design.  This chapter will cover the independent-samples t test which compares two sample means to test for significant difference, the paired samples t test which compares two sample means that are paired in some way.*

# SPSS FOR RESEARCH METHODS

## A Basic Guide

# AN INTRODUCTION TO SPSS

I have been teaching Research Methods and Statistics classes for nearly 20 years, and I have learned that analyzing and interpreting data is one of the hardest (and potentially scariest) tasks that you will be asked to master. Although data analysis may seem overwhelming at first, I have learned that you will be most successful when the instructions you are following are clear and to the point. This IBM® SPSS® Statistics software ("SPSS")[1] guide, *SPSS for Research Methods: A Basic Guide,* is designed to provide you the basics of data analysis and interpretation in a clear-cut and succinct way. I try to provide just enough information for you to accomplish the task at hand. This is not a research methods or statistics textbook, but rather a companion to your text that will help guide you through data analysis and interpretation using SPSS. Why SPSS? There are several other great data analysis packages out there, but SPSS is a very commonly used package that is tailored to the kind of analyses we use in the social sciences.

I have used sample data that are similar to the kind of data that you will likely be collecting in your research methods class: nothing too fancy or complicated. I have also used examples that my students have been interested in testing over the past few years in my research methods class, such as how having a tattoo makes people think the person is less intelligent or how being more motivated increases your GPA.

An important part of being a competent researcher using SPSS is that you are able to interpret the output that SPSS provides and turn that output into a Results section written in APA style. For each analysis that is covered in this guide, I will interpret the output and then give you an example of how you might write those results in an APA-style research paper. Of course, there are many ways to write about results, but I will provide you an example of one way to accomplish that well.

I follow a format starting in Chapter 2 where all information is presented in the following way:

1. I will show you what example data were used for each chapter, including how the data look entered into SPSS.

2. I will introduce the data analysis technique in general terms.

---

[1] SPSS Inc. was acquired by IBM in October, 2009.

3. In a section called *SPSS Commands* I will tell you how to command SPSS to run each analysis to give you the output you want.

4. In a section called *SPSS Output* I will show you the SPSS output that you will get from those commands.

5. In a section called *Interpretation* I will tell you how to interpret that SPSS output.

6. In a section called *APA Style* I will illustrate how to report the interpretation of data in APA style.

The commands and output are illustrated using screen shots so that you can see exactly what your screen will look like as you are doing your analyses. I hope this guide helps make data analysis a bit less scary and easier to accomplish well.

But before any analysis can be done, you first have to get your data into SPSS. So let's begin!

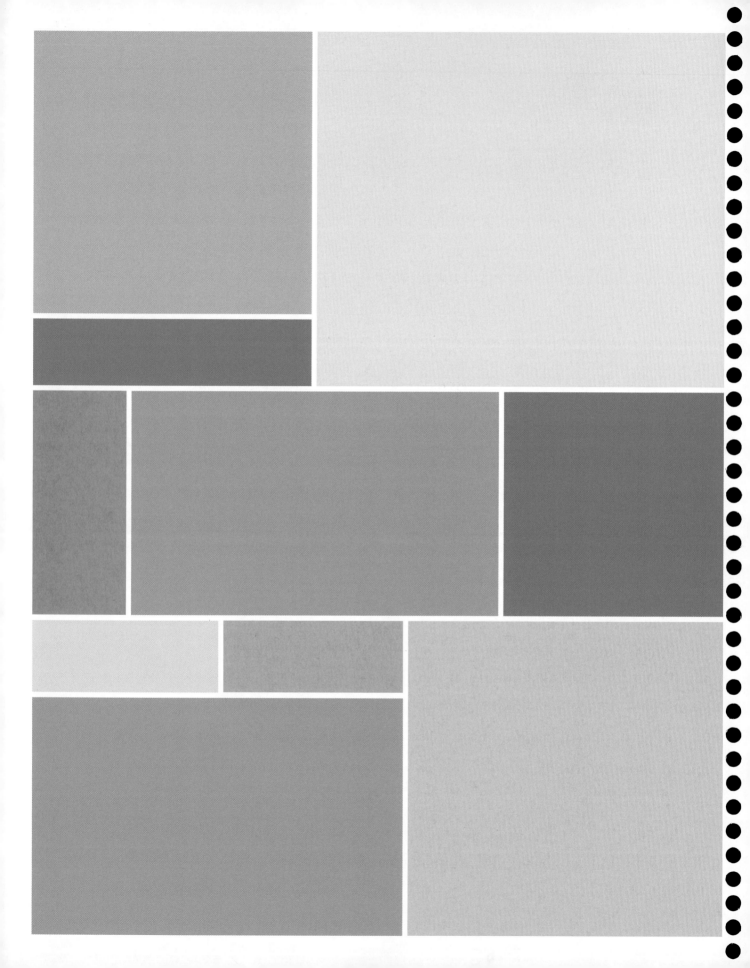

# 1

# SPSS Data Entry Basics

*This chapter introduces you to the SPSS environment (e.g., different windows), walks you through the basics of creating or importing a data set in SPSS, then shows you the basics of data setup.*

## Before We Get Started: Navigating in SPSS

SPSS is a basic "point and click" spreadsheet program. Using navigation bars along the top menu bar and drop-down menus, you can easily accomplish a desired data analysis. I used SPSS version 21 in this book, but these commands don't change radically over the different versions of SPSS. I also used screen shots from the PC version of SPSS. The MAC version is very similar with some minor changes in locations of tabs, but you shouldn't have any trouble finding what you need regardless of which version you are using. Below are some SPSS basics to get you acclimated to the program.

## 1.1 Windows in SPSS

There are two important windows in SPSS that you will need to be familiar with: the Data Window and the Output Window. The two windows contain different information with the Data Window containing the raw data that you type in or import from another source, and the Output Window containing the results of every command you give to SPSS, including all of your statistical tables and graphs called "output." The Data Window will be the first window that opens in SPSS, and after you run your first command (like saving the data you enter or telling SPSS to make a graph) the Output Window will appear. There is a third window called the Syntax Window where you can save a log of all the commands you tell SPSS to do through the point and click menus. The Syntax Window is not automatic, but later in this chapter I will mention how to save your commands into the Syntax Window if you choose.

## 1.1a The Data Window

The Data Window is where you set up and enter data in a spreadsheet. There are two views in the Data Window, and you can toggle between these two views by clicking the tab on the lower part of your screen. The *Data View* is where you can see all of your raw data entered in by case with the variable names across the top. The *Variable View* is where you set up your data by telling SPSS important information about each variable that you enter. Here's an example of each of these windows.

### Data Window

**Data View**

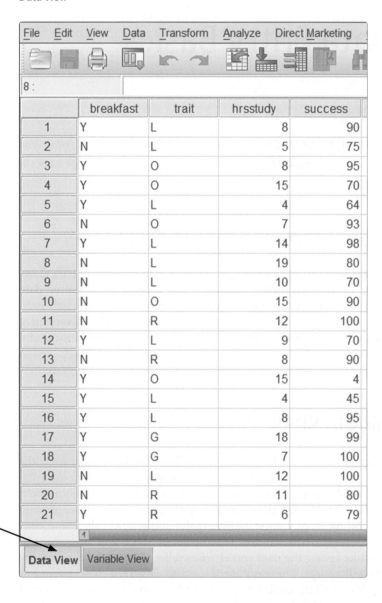

**Variable View**

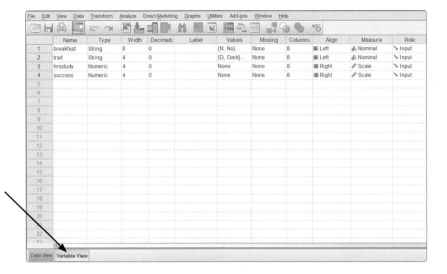

When saving data from the Data Window, the file will have .sav after the name you give it and that will tell you that it is a data file. For example, this data could be named *chapter1data.sav*.

## 1.1b The Output Window

The second important window is the Output Window. The Output Window displays a running record of all tasks you command SPSS to accomplish as well as the graphs and results of analyses you run.

**Output Window**

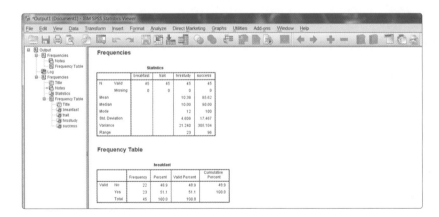

When saving output from the Output Window, the file will have .spv after the name you give it and that will tell you that it is an output file. For example, this output of frequencies could be named *chapter1data.spv*.

## 1.1c  Syntax Window

Whenever you tell SPSS to accomplish a task, we call that "running a command." You can keep a log of all the commands you tell SPSS to run by saving them into the Syntax Window. At the end of each series of commands you tell SPSS, right before you click **OK** , you can click **Paste** and the commands will be saved into a new window called the Syntax Window. The Syntax Window can help you keep track of the analyses you run so you can run them again in the same way and understand what commands led to your output.

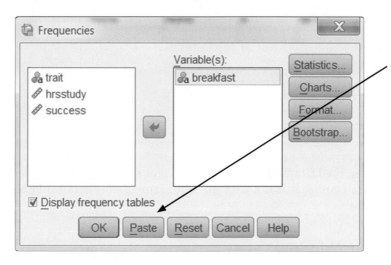

When you paste your commands into the Syntax Window this is what that window will look like. You can simply save this window to have a log of all commands you run. You can also run analyses from this window by highlighting the commands you want to run and clicking the ▶ button.

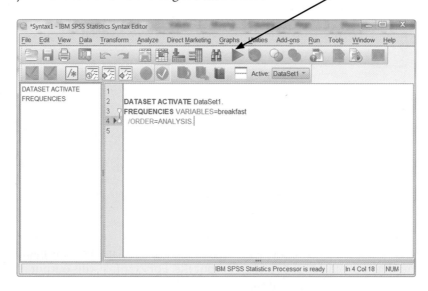

## 1.2 Navigating and Commands in SPSS

In each window there are several ways to command SPSS to accomplish tasks. The Top Menu Bar is where you will find drop-down menus to open and save your data or output, compute and recode variables, run all analyses, and graph your data. We will use the Top Menu Bar whenever there are instructions on how to accomplish tasks in SPSS.

**Top Menu Bar**

Another common way to navigate SPSS is through pop-up windows. Often, when you select a command from the Top Menu Bar a pop-up window will appear. In these pop-up windows you can tell SPSS which variables you are working with and what type of analysis you would like SPSS to run. These pop-up windows often have buttons that pull up other pop-up windows for more detailed and customized analyses. All pop-up window commands are executed by pressing the **OK** button when you have specified the analysis you want SPSS to run.

**Pop-Up Windows**

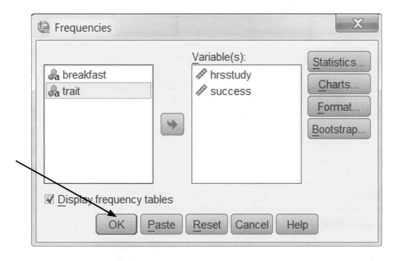

## 1.3 Importing Data from Other Sources

Often times we have data that have been collected from other sources like data entered into Excel or collected using online survey software. These data are easily transferred into SPSS for data analysis.

## 1.3a   Importing Data from Excel

If you have data that have been collected and entered into Microsoft Excel, you can easily import that data and keep the formatting by following these instructions.

Select from the Top Menu Bar:

$$FILE \rightarrow OPEN \rightarrow DATA$$

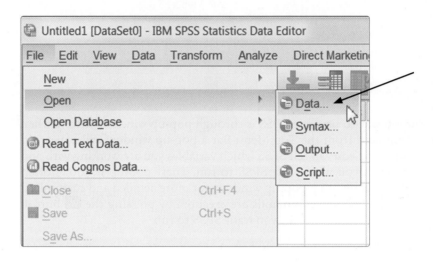

In the *Open Data* pop-up window, change *Files of type* to Excel and then select the Excel file you want to import as the *File name*, then click **Open**.

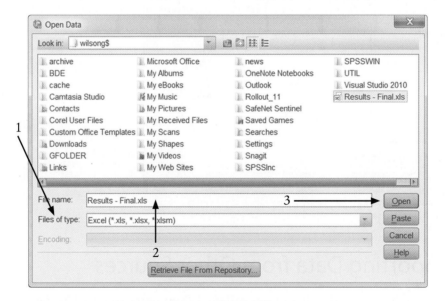

In the *Opening Excel Data Source* pop-up window, be sure to select the checkbox that says *Read variable names from the first row of data* if you have variable names as the top row of your Excel worksheet; if not, then do not select that option. Then click OK.

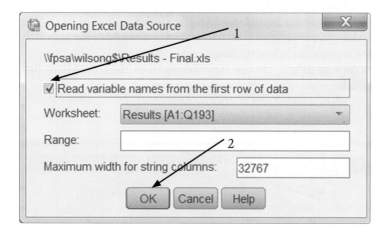

This is what your data should look like in the SPSS Data Window with the variable names across the top in blue and the data in rows by case. SPSS will sometimes alter the variable names when the data are imported so don't be alarmed if the names are condensed or changed. Also, always check over your data to be sure they look the way they should after importing.

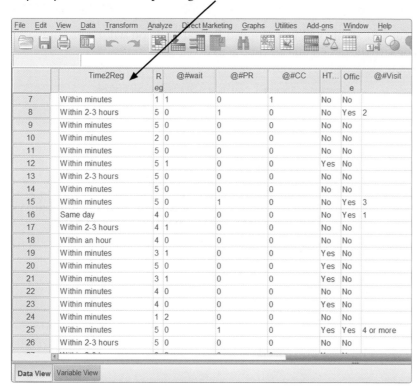

### 1.3b Importing Data from Online Survey Software: Example—Qualtrics

If you would like to import data from online survey software (e.g., Qualtrics or SurveyMonkey), the import has to be initiated in the survey software itself. For example, in Qualtrics, there is a *Download Data* tool that will download data directly into SPSS format using these simple instructions.

First, in Qualtrics (not in SPSS), choose *View Results* from the Top Menu Bar, then choose ⬇ *Download Data* .

Then, in the next window under *Format*: choose *Download SPSS.sav File*. Like this:

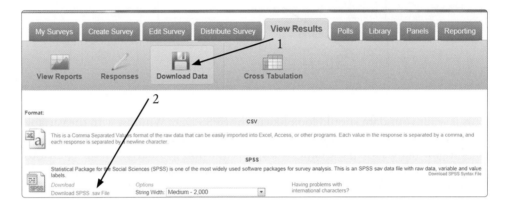

The downloaded SPSS file will be in zipped format and you will be prompted to either open or save the data. You can choose to do either.

# 1.4 Data Setup and Manual Entry

If your data are not already entered into Excel or collected through an online survey software then you will manually enter data—what SPSS calls "Type in data."

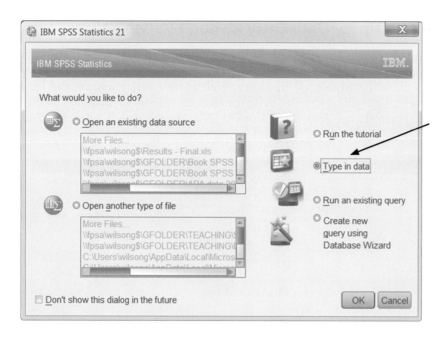

When we manually enter in data, we set up the data file first in the Data Window in *Variable View* and then manually type in the data in *Data View* (see Section 1.1 for an explanation of *Variable View* and *Data View* in the Data Window).

## THE DATA

In this data entry example, we will use data collected from the 45 students in my research methods class. A survey asked them the following questions:

1. **Do you typically eat breakfast on weekdays?**

   YES                           NO

2. **The personality trait that best describes me is (please circle only one):**

   Outgoing        Go-getter        Dark        Loving        Reserved        Intellectual

3. **In an average week, how many hours do you spend altogether doing the following: studying, reading school related materials, and doing homework?**

   _____ **hours**

4. **On a scale of 0% to 100%, how confident are you that you will be successful in life?**

   _____ **%**

## 1.4a   Setting Up for Data Entry through *Variable View*

You are going to set up your spreadsheet before entering in data so that the data are in a format that is understandable and accurate. In *Variable View*, you will set up your data file with variable specifications, such as your variable name and level of measurement. You will learn what to do for each column in *Variable View* below.

After you have selected *Type in data* from SPSS's opening screen, select the *Variable View* tab at the lower part of the window.

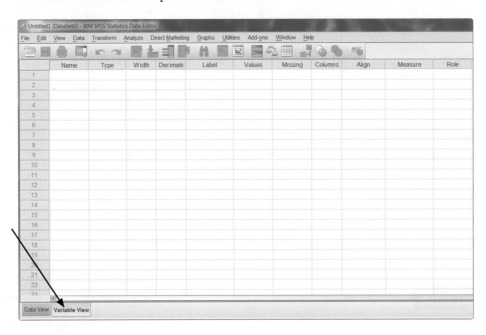

The Variable View window will be blank and you will go column by column to fill in the information like the example given here.

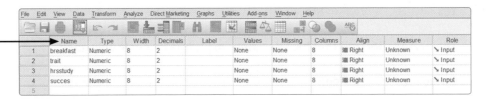

The first column (*Name*) is where you name each variable that you are going to enter. These names cannot have spaces or any special characters. You should try to abbreviate the variables—for example, "how many hours do you study in a week" can be abbreviated as *hrsstudy*. Because SPSS won't allow spaces or characters, you will have to be inventive about your variable names so they make sense to you without using any special characters like "#" or spaces like "hours study."

The second column (*Type*) is where you identify the type of data you have. You will be choosing either *String* (categorical, word/letter data) or *Numeric* (number data). If your data have letters or words (e.g., F for female and M for male) assigned to them you should choose *String*, while data with numbers assigned to them should be *Numeric*. Do note that SPSS will not run any statistics except for frequencies if you choose to enter your data as *String*. This makes sense because the levels of measurement of *String* data are nominal and ordinal and cannot be used in most quantitative analyses.

The third column (*Width*) tells SPSS how many characters long you want to allow for your data. SPSS has a default of 8 characters, which is fine for most data, although numeric data could have a shorter width so you can see more data at one time on the page.

The fourth column (*Decimals*) is where you specify how many places past the decimal point you would like SPSS to display for numeric variables. Because these example numeric variables are all whole numbers, the decimal places should be changed to 0 by clicking on the *Decimals* cell for *hrsstudy* and then clicking the down arrow to reduce the decimals to 0. If you have data that are accurate to the tenth you should chose decimals equal to 1, for data that are accurate to the hundredths you should choose decimals equal to 2, and so on. Do note that SPSS retains additional decimal data beyond what you choose to display in order to preserve accuracy in calculations using those variables.

| | Name | Type | Width | Decimals | |
|---|---|---|---|---|---|
| 1 | breakfast | String | 8 | 0 | |
| 2 | trait | String | 4 | 0 | |
| 3 | hrsstudy | Numeric | 4 | 2 | |
| 4 | succes | Numeric | 4 | 0 | |

The fifth column (*Label*) allows you to give the variable a full name like "*Do you typically eat breakfast on weekdays?*" instead of just the short name *Breakfast*. This can be helpful if you have a hard time with shortened variable names, but most of the time not typing in a label and just using the variable name is fine.

The sixth column (*Values*) allows you to provide value labels for letters or numbers that stand for longer values. For example, for the variable *Breakfast*, the values N and Y were used when the data were typed in, but we want SPSS to print out the value labels "No" and "Yes" in the output. Assigning value labels is especially helpful if you have several categories and you would like SPSS to print out the full name of each category rather than just a single letter or number. To assign value labels to a variable you click on the [...] button under *Values* for that variable.

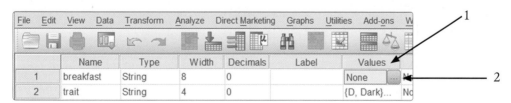

In the *Value Labels* pop-up window, type in the value that you will type when entering in the data under *Value*, and then the label you want it to be called under *Label*, then choose Add. Repeat this for each value label. Be sure to add all value labels, then click OK.

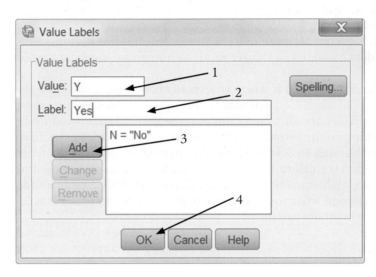

In the seventh column (*Missing*) you can identify a value which you will use to represent data that are missing if you don't want to just leave the cell blank when entering data. Be sure that you specify a number that is not a possible valid value and that can only be possible if the data are missing. For instance, if your variable has values between 1 and 10, then perhaps choose 99 as your missing value because 99 is not a possible valid value for your variable. To specify a value to stand for missing, select the *Missing* cell and then, in the *Missing Values* pop-up window, select *Discrete missing values* and type in the number you want to use (I specified 99).

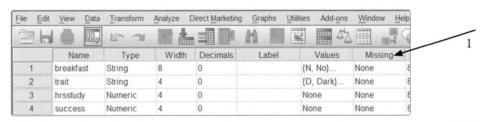

In the eighth and ninth columns are some preference choices for how you want your data to be displayed in data view. *Columns* refers to how many characters wide the column will display and *Align* refers to where you want the data displayed within each cell. These choices are individual preferences and do not affect the data at all. If you are fine with the default settings, then you can just leave them as they are.

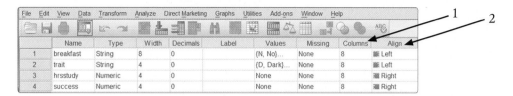

The last column of importance is the tenth column (*Measure*), which corresponds to the level of measurement of your data. There are three choices: *Nominal*, *Ordinal*, and *Scale*. *Nominal* refers to categorical (*String*) data that are not ranked or ordered (e.g., the *breakfast* or *trait* variables), *Ordinal* refers to data that are ranked (e.g., a Likert-scale items), and *Scale* refers to quantitative, numeric data including both interval and ratio levels of measurement (e.g., the *hrsstudy* or *success* variables). You can select the measure by clicking in the cell and selecting the appropriate choice from the dropdown menu.

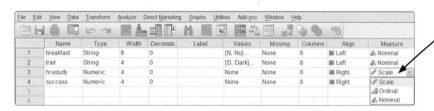

After everything is all set in *Variable View*, you should save your data by going to the Top Menu Bar:

FILE → SAVE AS

Then choose where you want to save the file and what you would like to call your data set. SPSS will automatically put the .sav after your file name to signify that this is a data file.

## 1.4b   Manual Data Entry in *Data View*

Once you have set up your SPSS data file in *Variable View* and saved it, then you are ready to enter data. To manually enter data you must switch to *Data View* by clicking on the tab at the bottom of your screen. You will see all of the variable names across the top and you will enter in each case across the rows. Be sure to save often as you are entering in data! It is always good practice to number your surveys or data sheets before entering the data just in case there is a question about something you entered. When your surveys are numbered, you can return to any particular survey to address any questions that may have come up.

| | breakfast | trait | hrsstudy | success |
|---|---|---|---|---|
| 1 | Y | L | 8 | 90 |
| 2 | N | L | 5 | 75 |
| 3 | Y | O | 8 | 95 |
| 4 | Y | O | 15 | 70 |
| 5 | Y | L | 4 | 64 |
| 6 | N | O | 7 | 93 |
| 7 | Y | L | 14 | 98 |
| 8 | N | L | 19 | 80 |
| 9 | N | L | 10 | 70 |
| 10 | N | O | 15 | 90 |
| 11 | N | R | 12 | 100 |
| 12 | Y | L | 9 | 70 |
| 13 | N | R | 8 | 90 |
| 14 | Y | O | 15 | 4 |
| 15 | Y | L | 4 | 45 |
| 16 | Y | L | 8 | 95 |
| 17 | Y | G | 18 | 99 |
| 18 | Y | G | 7 | 100 |
| 19 | N | L | 12 | 100 |
| 20 | N | R | 11 | 80 |
| 21 | Y | R | 6 | 79 |

**File   Edit   View   Data   Transform   Analyze   Direct Marketing**

**Data View   Variable View**

# 1.5 Data Transformation

After your data are entered, there may be a need to change your data in some form, such as recoding values or adding variables together to create a new summed variable that is a scale. For example, it is very common to ask several questions about the same concept, such as asking several questions about a person's sense of community instead of just one question. When asking a series of questions about the same concept it is typical to have some of the questions positively worded and some negatively worded. For example, we might ask how much agreement a person has on a 5-point Likert-scale with the positive statement, "I feel as though I belong in this neighborhood," as well as how much agreement a person has with the negative statement, "I feel as though there is no one in my neighborhood who shares the same values as I do." If we were going to create a sense of community scale by adding together the Likert-scaled responses for these two statements and others as well, we would want to be sure that a larger value for agreement means a more positive sense of community for all the items. That would mean we would have to flip (reverse code) the values of negatively stated items, such as the second statement above, so that a higher number would correspond with a more positive sense of community rather than a more negative sense of community. Then when we add together the values, a larger sum means a more positive sense of community. These changes to data are called "data transformations," and they are an important part of getting your data ready to be analyzed. This section will cover the two most common types of data transformations: recoding values and computing a new variable.

## THE DATA

We will use example variables from data collected from the 45 students in my research methods class. A survey asked them to circle the best-fitting answer to the following Likert-scale questions regarding the class:

1. **The material we cover in this class is easy for me to understand.**

   Strongly Disagree      Disagree      Neutral      Agree      Strongly Agree

2. **There is a good chance that I will receive a low grade in this class.**

   Strongly Disagree      Disagree      Neutral      Agree      Strongly Agree

3. **I am confident that I will be successful in this class.**

   Strongly Disagree      Disagree      Neutral      Agree      Strongly Agree

4. **I am often confused after learning something new in this class.**

   Strongly Disagree      Disagree      Neutral      Agree      Strongly Agree

5. **I know my grade in this class will be higher than my classmates.**

   Strongly Disagree      Disagree      Neutral      Agree      Strongly Agree

## 1.5a Recoding Values

The first type of data transformation is recoding a variable's answer values. There are instances, very often when using Likert-scale items, when you may need to recode (flip) that variable's values. For this example (see questions above), we are using a 5-point Likert-scale items about opinions of the Research Methods class and we would like to add up the responses to the five items. Three of the items were positively worded (*Likert1*, *Likert3*, and *Likert5*), and two of the items were negatively worded (*Likert2* and *Likert4*) and will need to have their values flipped or recoded (called "reverse coded") before we can add them together. In this way, a higher value would represent a more positive opinion regardless of how the item was stated.

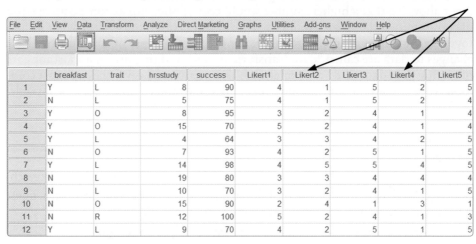

| | breakfast | trait | hrsstudy | success | Likert1 | Likert2 | Likert3 | Likert4 | Likert5 |
|---|---|---|---|---|---|---|---|---|---|
| 1 | Y | L | 8 | 90 | 4 | 1 | 5 | 2 | 5 |
| 2 | N | L | 5 | 75 | 4 | 1 | 5 | 2 | 4 |
| 3 | Y | O | 8 | 95 | 3 | 2 | 4 | 1 | 4 |
| 4 | Y | O | 15 | 70 | 5 | 2 | 4 | 1 | 4 |
| 5 | Y | L | 4 | 64 | 3 | 3 | 4 | 2 | 5 |
| 6 | N | O | 7 | 93 | 4 | 2 | 5 | 1 | 5 |
| 7 | Y | L | 14 | 98 | 4 | 5 | 5 | 4 | 5 |
| 8 | N | L | 19 | 80 | 3 | 3 | 4 | 4 | 4 |
| 9 | N | L | 10 | 70 | 3 | 2 | 4 | 1 | 5 |
| 10 | N | O | 15 | 90 | 2 | 4 | 1 | 3 | 1 |
| 11 | N | R | 12 | 100 | 5 | 2 | 4 | 1 | 3 |
| 12 | Y | L | 9 | 70 | 4 | 2 | 5 | 1 | 5 |

*Likert1*, *Likert3*, and *Likert5* responses were entered where *Strongly Agree* is a strong positive opinion and has been coded as a 5, but notice how *Likert2* and *Likert4* were negatively worded where *Strongly Agree* is a strong negative opinion and has been coded as a 5. We will need to recode those values in reverse because we entered in the answers just as they were circled on the survey. We now need to flip the responses to be consistent with the other three items where a 5 represents a strong positive opinion. So we will need to reverse code *Likert2* and *Likert4* by recoding 1 as a 5, 2 as a 4, 5 as a 1, 4 as a 2, and leave 3 as a neutral 3.

To recode a variable (e.g., *Likert2*), select from the Top Menu Bar:

TRANSFORM → RECODE INTO DIFFERENT VARIABLES

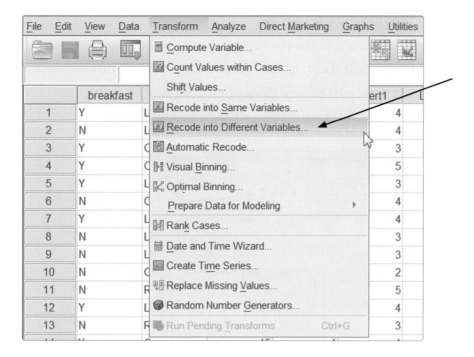

In the *Recode into Different Variables* pop-up window,

    1—Double-click *Likert2* into the *Numeric Variable* window

    2—*Name* your Output variable (I called it *Likert2R* for *Likert2* recoded.)

    3—*Label* your Output variable (I called it *Reverse coded Likert2*.)

    4—Then select Old and New Values

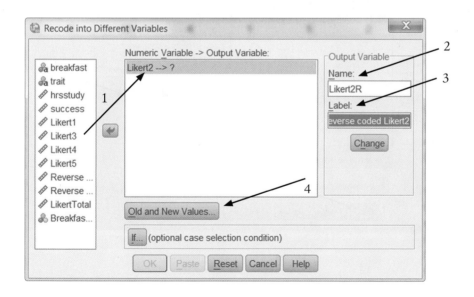

In the *Old and New Values* pop-up window,

> 1—Type the old value (i.e., 5) under *Value* in the *Old Value* window

> 2—Type the new value (i.e., 1) under *Value* in the *New Value* window

> 3—Click Add after each Old-New Value pair you enter in

> 4—When you have added each Old-New Value pair, click Continue

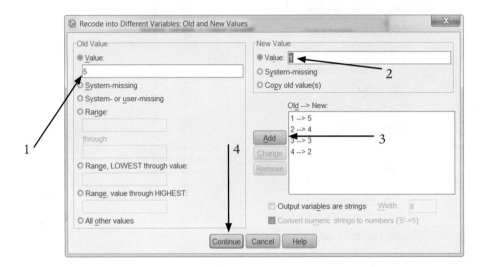

When you return to the *Recode into Different Variables* window, click Change, then OK.

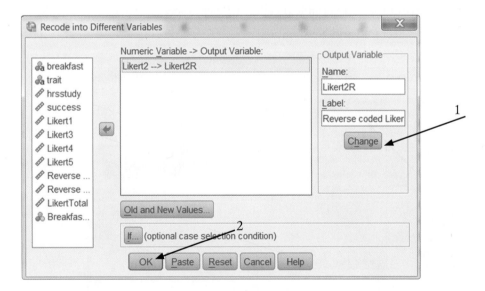

## 1.5b  Collapsing or Combining Values

Another common type of data transformation is collapsing values into fewer categories, which is accomplished by recoding ranges of values instead of one-to-one recodes. For instance, if we wanted to recode *Strongly Disagree* and *Disagree* as one value (e.g., 1), *Neutral* as one category (e.g., 2), and *Agree* and *Strongly Agree* as one category (e.g., 3), we could accomplish this using *Recode into Different Variables*.

To recode *Likert2* from a 5-category variable into a 3-category reverse-coded variable, select from the Top Menu Bar:

TRANSFORM → RECODE INTO DIFFERENT VARIABLES

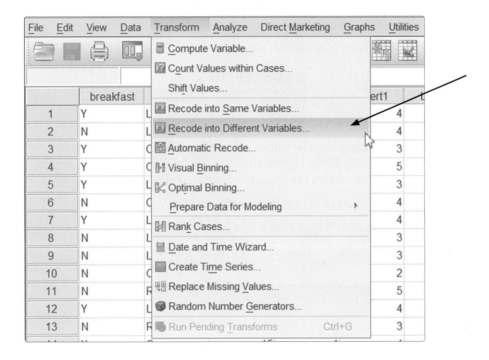

In the *Recode into Different Variables* pop-up window,

    1—Double-click *Likert2* into the *Numeric Variable* window

    2—*Name* your Output variable (I called it *Likert2R* for *Likert2* recoded.)

    3—*Label* your Output variable (I called it Reverse coded Likert2 in
       3 categories.)

    4—Then select Old and New Values

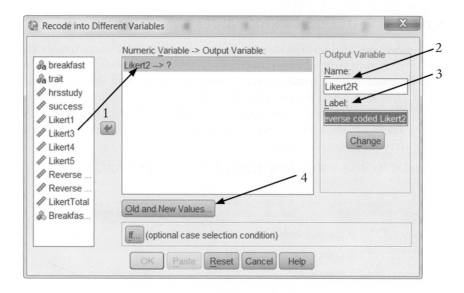

In the *Old and New Values* pop-up window,

>   1—Type the lowest and highest values under *Range* (i.e., lowest value = 4, highest value = 5). Note: For the middle value of 3, I entered that as an Old Value rather than a range as demonstrated above.
>
>   2—Type the new value (i.e., 1) under *Value* in the New Value Window
>
>   3—Click Add after each Range-New Value pair
>
>   4—When you have added each Range-New Value pair, click Continue

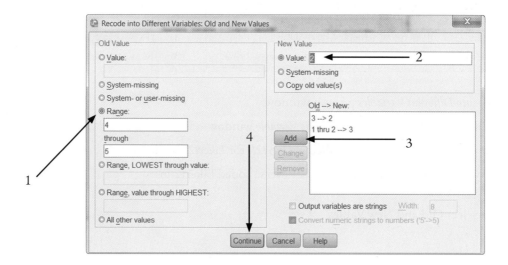

When you return to the *Recode into Different Variables* window, click **Change**, then **OK**.

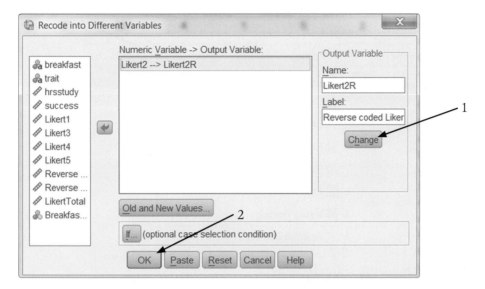

## 1.5c   Computing Summative Scales

The third common type of data transformation is computing a new variable, particularly a variable that is the sum of several items to create a scale. This type of data transformation can compute a total quiz score, a sense of community combined score, or a depression index score for multiple depression items. In our example, we may want to create a "research methods class opinion scale" by adding together the five Likert-scale questions (making sure *Likert2* and *Likert4* are recoded before adding them). This will create a summed score of positive opinions about the research methods class (let's call it *LikertTotal*).

To create a summative scale, select from the Top Menu Bar:

TRANSFORM → COMPUTE VARIABLE

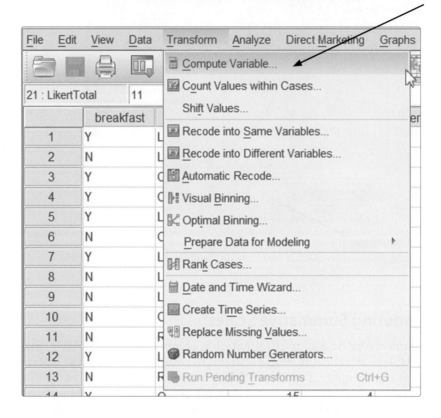

In the *Compute Variable* pop-up window,

1—Name the Target Variable (I called the sum of the 5 Likert-scale items *LikertTotal*.)

2—One by one, move the items to the *Numeric Expression* window (Note that I selected *Likert2R* and *Likert4R* because they were already reverse coded. See Section 1.5a for instructions on recoding variables.)

3—After each item is moved to the *Numeric Expression* window, select the plus sign to add each item

4—When you have added all the items, click **OK**. SPSS will compute the summed scale for all cases and then add this new variable, *LikertTotal*, to the data set.

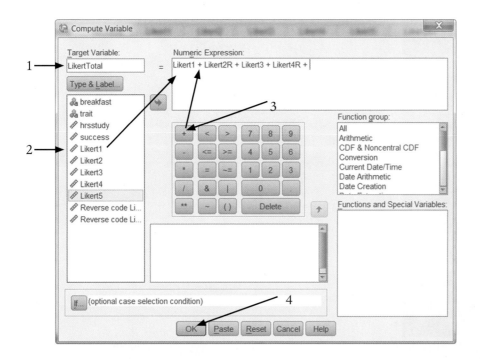

If you were to write about this newly created summed scale in an APA-style paper, this information would likely appear in the Method section. Here is an example of how you might present this new summed variable in APA style:

We measured positive opinions about the research methods class using a summed scale of five items coded on a 5-point scale (1 = *Strongly Disagree* to 5 = *Strongly Agree*). Two of the five items were reverse-coded before computing the summed scale called the *Positive Opinions about Research Methods Scale* (PORMS). The PORMS scores ranged from 5 to 25 ($M = 17.40$, $SD = 3.96$).

# 2

## Getting a Feel for Your Data

### Descriptive Statistics

*The first step in any research project is getting a good sense of the main qualities of the data. In this chapter, you will learn how to use IBM SPSS Statistics software ("SPSS") to compute basic descriptive statistics focusing on the most common statistics and ways to illustrate the data.*

**THE DATA**

In this chapter, we will use the same example variables that we used in the first part of Chapter 1 from data collected from the 45 students in my research methods class. A survey asked them the following questions:

1. **Do you typically eat breakfast on weekdays?**

   YES                    NO

2. **The personality trait that best describes me is (please circle only one):**

   Outgoing        Go-getter        Dark        Loving        Reserved        Intellectual

3. **In an average week, how many hours do you spend altogether doing the following: studying, reading school related materials, and doing homework?**

   **hours** _____

4. **On a scale of 0% to 100%, how confident are you that you will be successful in life?**

   **%** _____

# Using Descriptive Statistics

It can be overwhelming looking through column after column of raw data like this after you enter it into SPSS or import it from Excel or survey software (see Chapter 1).

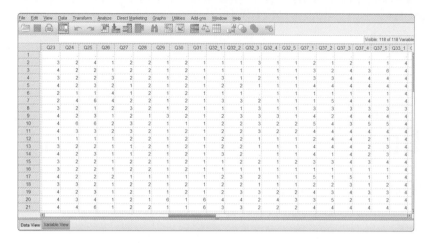

That is where our first step in statistical analysis comes into play. Using descriptive statistics in the form of frequency tables, graphs, and statistics that show central tendency (e.g., mean and median) and variability (e.g., range and standard deviation) helps us to organize and summarize this massive amount of data.

# Before We Get Started: Identify Your Variable Type

As we talked about in Chapter 1, there are two main types of data: categorical (*String*) data and quantitative (*Numeric*) data. How these two types of data are analyzed is very different, so be sure to use the correct analysis for your data. For example, you cannot calculate a mean or run a *t* test on *String* data that are nominal or ordinal, so you need to think about your variable type and be sure it is correct before you begin analysis. You should also be sure that you have identified each variable's type and set up your data correctly when you entered or imported the data before beginning any analyses (see Section 1.4a for instructions for data setup).

# Frequency Tables and Basic Graphs

When we first take a look at our data, we want to get a general picture of what the data look like. Using frequency tables and graphs allows us to do that. With one simple SPSS command we are able to see the frequencies of the different values of the variables in the data set.

# 2.1 Categorical Data: Describing Our Data with Frequency Tables and Graphs

Frequency tables and graphs are a great way to describe categorical data, but be aware that there are some choices about types of graphs to use for this type of data. When your data are categorical, bar graphs are the best type of graph to choose because the gaps or spaces between the bars on the graph represent that each value is a separate word or category.

In our SPSS example, we have a categorical variable that we could describe with a frequency table and a bar graph: personality trait (named *trait*). Here's how to get the frequency table and bar graph using SPSS.

Select from the Top Menu Bar:

*SPSS Commands*
**2.1**

ANALYZE → DESCRIPTIVE STATISTICS → FREQUENCIES

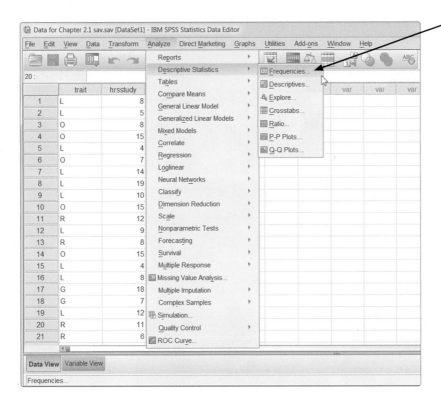

In the *Frequencies* pop-up window, double-click or drag *trait* from the left-hand side into the *Variables* box, then click the Charts... button.

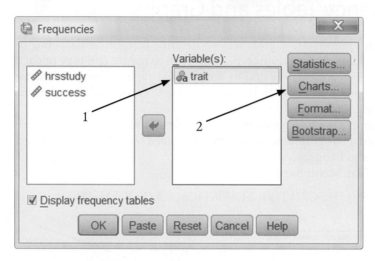

In the *Frequencies: Charts* pop-up window, select *Bar charts* from the choices listed, then click Continue, then click OK.

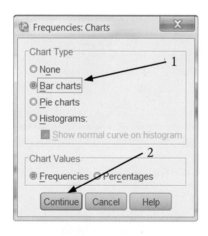

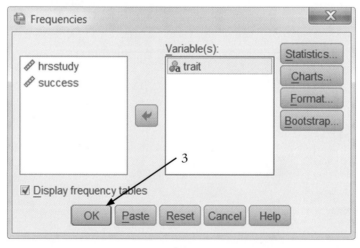

When you complete this command, this is the frequency table and bar graph that SPSS produces:

## Frequencies

| | | Frequency | Percent | Valid Percent | Cumulative Percent |
|---|---|---|---|---|---|
| | | | | trait | |
| Valid | Dark | 1 | 2.2 | 2.2 | 2.2 |
| | Go-getter | 3 | 6.7 | 6.7 | 8.9 |
| | Intellectual | 2 | 4.4 | 4.4 | 13.3 |
| | Loving | 19 | 42.2 | 42.2 | 55.6 |
| | Outgoing | 14 | 31.1 | 31.1 | 86.7 |
| | Reserved | 6 | 13.3 | 13.3 | 100.0 |
| | Total | 45 | 100.0 | 100.0 | |

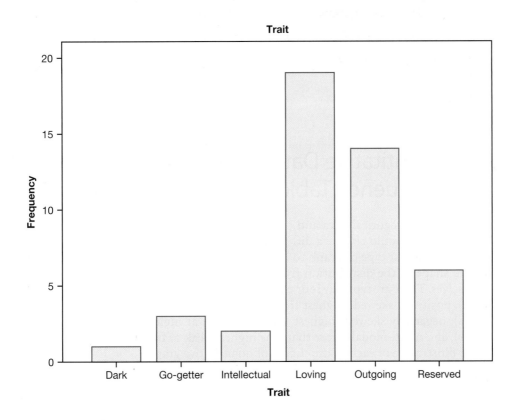

*Interpretation*
**2.1**

The frequency table and the graph together tell us a story about this categorical variable. According to the frequency table for personality trait, it looks like students in the class most frequently report having loving and outgoing personalities. You can also use the valid percent column to report these same values in percentages instead of frequencies. For example, we might say that 42% of my students would say that *loving* is the personality trait that best describes them, followed by 31% describing themselves as *outgoing*. In general, it would seem that a large percentage of the students describe themselves with positive personality traits.

*APA Style*
**2.1**

It would be most likely that you would use this type of frequency data in describing the sample in the Participants section of the Method section of an APA-style paper. You would use the valid percent to report this data producing a paragraph that might look like this:

As a part of their end-of-semester course evaluations, 45 undergraduate psychology majors who had taken a research methods class volunteered to participate in this study. Participants selected the personality trait that best described them from a list of six choices (e.g., *loving*). Forty-two percent of respondents chose *loving* as the personality trait that best described them, 31.1% selected *outgoing*, 13.3% selected *reserved*, and less than 10% chose one of the other three traits: *go-getter, intellectual,* or *dark.*

## 2.2 Quantitative Data: Describing Our Data with Frequency Tables and Graphs

Compared to categorical data and the use of a bar graph, when you have quantitative data you would choose a different graph to best illustrate your data. Histograms are the best type of graph to describe quantitative variables because we can see the shape of the distribution from the graph as well as from the frequencies themselves. There are typically four common shapes of graphs: normal (bell-shaped curve), positively skewed (highest frequencies are at low values with fewer at high values), negatively skewed (highest frequencies are at high values with fewer low values), and multi-modal (more than one highest peak of frequency). See Table 2.1 for an illustration of each of the shapes of quantitative graphs.

**Table 2.1   Shapes of Quantitative Graphs of Frequency Distributions**

1. Normal—bell-shaped curve, symmetrical with most responses in the middle and fewer responses on the tails. (Example: height, grades on a curve)

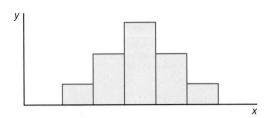

Note: You can fold this graph in half and both sides would be equal.

2. Positively Skewed—most values are low with a few high values (tail pulled to positive side). (Example: income)

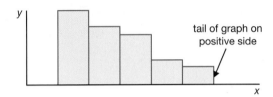

tail of graph on positive side

3. Negatively Skewed—most values are high with a few low values (tail pulled toward negative side). (Example: age at retirement)

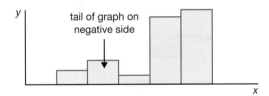

tail of graph on negative side

4. Multi-Modal—more than one highest peak. (Example: shoe size)

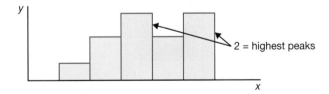

2 = highest peaks

We will use the frequency table and the histogram to help us get a preliminary feel for what our data look like. In our SPSS example, we have two quantitative variables that we could describe with a frequency table and a histogram: hours studied in a typical week (named *hrsstudy*) and confidence of success (named *success*). Here's how to get a frequency table and histogram using SPSS.

Select from the Top Menu Bar:

ANALYZE → DESCRIPTIVE STATISTICS → FREQUENCIES

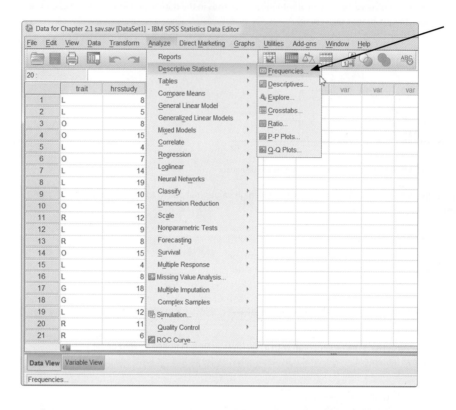

In the *Frequencies* pop-up window, double-click or drag *hrsstudy* and *success* from the left-hand side into the *Variables* box, then click the **Charts...** button.

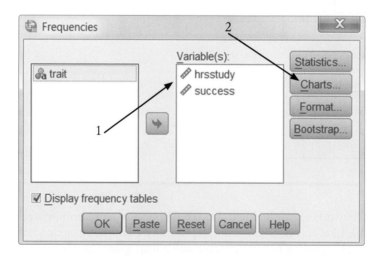

In the *Frequencies: Charts* pop-up window, select *Histograms* from the choices listed and check the box for *Show normal curve on histogram*, then click **Continue**, then click **OK**.

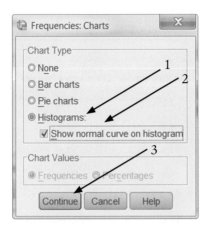

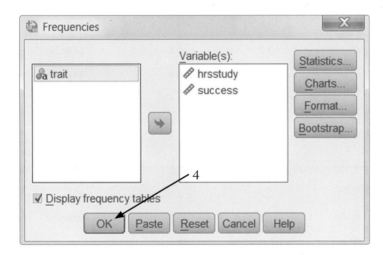

When you complete these commands, here's what you'll get from SPSS: a frequency table and a histogram for each of these variables in the Output Window.

## Frequency Table

| | | Frequency | Percent | Valid Percent | Cumulative Percent |
|---|---|---|---|---|---|
| | | | hrsstudy | | |
| Valid | 2 | 1 | 2.2 | 2.2 | 2.2 |
| | 4 | 2 | 4.4 | 4.4 | 6.7 |
| | 5 | 5 | 11.1 | 11.1 | 17.8 |
| | 6 | 2 | 4.4 | 4.4 | 22.2 |
| | 7 | 3 | 6.7 | 6.7 | 28.9 |
| | 8 | 5 | 11.1 | 11.1 | 40.0 |
| | 9 | 1 | 2.2 | 2.2 | 42.2 |
| | 10 | 5 | 11.1 | 11.1 | 53.3 |
| | 11 | 1 | 2.2 | 2.2 | 55.6 |
| | 12 | 9 | 20.0 | 20.0 | 75.6 |
| | 14 | 2 | 4.4 | 4.4 | 80.0 |
| | 15 | 5 | 11.1 | 11.1 | 91.1 |
| | 16 | 1 | 2.2 | 2.2 | 93.3 |
| | 18 | 1 | 2.2 | 2.2 | 95.6 |
| | 19 | 1 | 2.2 | 2.2 | 97.8 |
| | 25 | 1 | 2.2 | 2.2 | 100.0 |
| | Total | 45 | 100.0 | 100.0 | |

| success | | Frequency | Percent | Valid Percent | Cumulative Percent |
|---|---|---|---|---|---|
| Valid | 4 | 1 | 2.2 | 2.2 | 2.2 |
| | 45 | 1 | 2.2 | 2.2 | 4.4 |
| | 64 | 1 | 2.2 | 2.2 | 6.7 |
| | 66 | 1 | 2.2 | 2.2 | 8.9 |
| | 70 | 3 | 6.7 | 6.7 | 15.6 |
| | 75 | 2 | 4.4 | 4.4 | 20.0 |
| | 79 | 1 | 2.2 | 2.2 | 22.2 |
| | 80 | 4 | 8.9 | 8.9 | 31.1 |
| | 85 | 4 | 8.9 | 8.9 | 40.0 |
| | 88 | 2 | 4.4 | 4.4 | 44.4 |
| | 90 | 7 | 15.6 | 15.6 | 60.0 |
| | 93 | 1 | 2.2 | 2.2 | 62.2 |
| | 95 | 4 | 8.9 | 8.9 | 71.1 |
| | 98 | 1 | 2.2 | 2.2 | 73.3 |
| | 99 | 2 | 4.4 | 4.4 | 77.8 |
| | 100 | 10 | 22.2 | 22.2 | 100.0 |
| | Total | 45 | 100.0 | 100.0 | |

**Histogram**

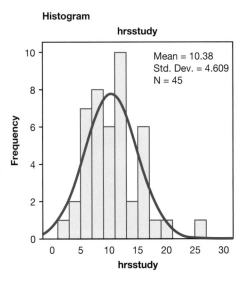

Mean = 10.38
Std. Dev. = 4.609
N = 45

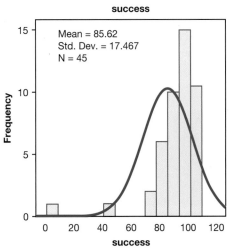

Mean = 85.62
Std. Dev. = 17.467
N = 45

As with categorical data, the frequency table and the graph together tell us a story about each quantitative variable. The frequency table has several columns that add information to our story. The first column shows the values of the variable such as the number of hours studied. The second column shows the frequency, or number of people, who responded with that value. The third and fourth columns show percentages with the valid percent being calculated without the inclusion of missing values in the total. The last column shows the cumulative percentage: the percent of the sample who report a certain value and all the values below that value. In our example, let's look at the *hrsstudy* variable. According to the frequency table under the frequency column, it looks like students in the class study between 2 and 25 hours per week with the highest frequency associated with 12 hours of studying per week. The next most frequently reported hours of studying include 5, 8, 10, and 15 hours studied. You can also use the valid percent column to report these same values in percentages instead of frequencies. For example, we might say that 20% of the students study 12 hours per week. From the cumulative percent column you can see that approximately 76% of the students study 12 hours or less. You can see from the histogram that the shape of the *hrsstudy* graph is positively skewed with some variations (selecting the *Show Normal Curve* option allows you to visually see what the shape would look like if it were normal). You will also note that SPSS has grouped the values on the x-axis (e.g., in the success graph the x-axis goes up by tens with the tick marks being labeled every 20) to make this graph more compact. You can always change that setting, but for the purposes of just looking at a graph for describing frequencies it doesn't seem necessary.

For our other variable, *how confident the student is that s/he will be successful in life* (called *success*), we find from the frequency table that confidence of success ranged from 4 all the way up to 100, with 100% confident being most frequently reported, followed by 90%. Using the valid percent, you could also say that approximately 22% of the students are 100% confident of their success. From the cumulative percent column, you can see that 60% of the students are 90% confident of their success or less. You can see from the histogram that the shape of this graph is negatively skewed, meaning that most of my students report high values of confidence of their success, and just a few students report low values of confidence of their future success.

Looking at the frequency table and the histogram give us a very general and preliminary idea about our data. It looks like the students study, for the most part, around 8 to 15 hours per week, and with a few exceptions, they are fairly confident that they will be successful in life.

Again, it would be most likely that you would use this type of frequency data in describing the sample in the Participants section of the Method section of an APA-style paper. You would use the valid percent to report this data in a paragraph that might look like this:

As a part of their end-of-semester course evaluations, 45 undergraduate psychology majors who had taken a research methods class volunteered to participate in this study. Participants answered a question about the number of hours they spent altogether studying, reading school related materials, and doing homework in an average week. Reponses ranged from two to 25 hours per week with the highest frequency being 12 hours per week (20%), followed by 5, 8, 10, and 15 hours, each accounting for 11% of the responses. Participants also reported how confident they were that they will be successful in life on a scale of 0% to 100%. Responses ranged from 4% to 100% with the most frequent answer being 100% confident, accounting for 22% of the responses.

## 2.3 Descriptive Statistics: Measures of Central Tendency and Variability for Quantitative Data

Descriptive statistics help us to both organize and summarize data. Organizing and summarizing data are important in allowing us to talk about the data in a way that is useful. Some ways to organize and summarize data that we already covered in this chapter were frequency tables and graphs. We also can summarize data, not just with a table or graph, but with a single value called a *descriptive statistic*. There are a number of descriptive statistics. These statistics summarize quantitative data in two ways: by measuring the central tendency (the "typical" response or the response at the center) and by measuring the variability (how spread out the responses are). Measures of central tendency measure how data "hang together." The three measures of central tendency we will talk about in this chapter are the mode, median, and mean. Measures of variability are sometimes called measures of "spread." They measure how far apart the data are or the differences in the responses. We call a set of responses to a question a "variable" because not every person answers in the same way; there is variability in the answers. We will talk about two measures of variability in this chapter: the range and the standard deviation.

Let's go back to our SPSS example and have SPSS compute these descriptive statistics for us on our two quantitative variables: *hrsstudy* and *success*.

We are going to repeat what we did for frequency tables and graphs in the SPSS Commands 2.1 section by selecting from the Top Menu Bar:

ANALYZE → DESCRIPTIVE STATISTICS → FREQUENCIES

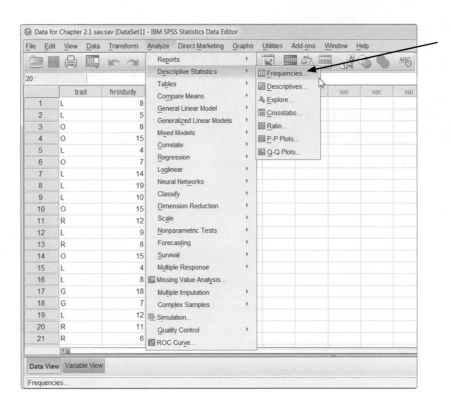

In the *Frequencies* pop-up window, double-click or drag *hrsstudy* and *success* from the left-hand side into the Variables box. This time, click the Statistics… button.

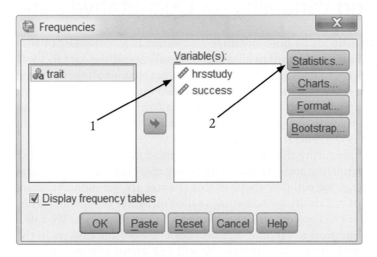

In the *Frequencies: Statistics* pop-up window, check *mean, median, mode, std. deviation,* and *range*, then click Continue, then click OK.

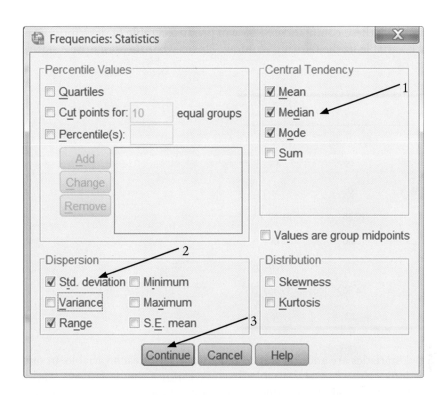

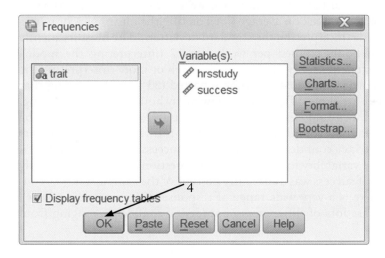

When you complete these commands, SPSS will produce a table of descriptive statistics for each variable in the Output Window. This is what the descriptive statistics look like:

**Statistics**

|  |  | hrsstudy | success |
|---|---|---|---|
| N | Valid | 45 | 45 |
|  | Missing | 0 | 0 |
| Mean |  | 10.38 | 85.62 |
| Median |  | 10.00 | 90.00 |
| Mode |  | 12 | 100 |
| Std. Deviation |  | 4.609 | 17.467 |
| Range |  | 23 | 96 |

The descriptive statistics are another way to tell a story about each variable. In our example, let's look at the *hrsstudy* variable first. We can use the descriptive statistics to tell us information about the amount of studying for this sample. Based on the descriptive statistics for how many hours per week the sample studies, the students study 10.4 hours per week on average (interpreting the mean) plus or minus 4.6 hours on either side (interpreting the standard deviation). The most frequently reported amount of hours studied per week was 12 (interpreting the mode). Fifty percent of the students study 10.4 hours per week or more (interpreting the median). There is a wide range in study time reported (23 hours), meaning that among students there are some differences in how many hours are spent studying.

In the same way, we could describe the *success* variable as well. Based on the descriptive statistics for how confident they are of their future success, the students report an average of 85.6% confidence in their future success plus or minus 17.5%, showing quite a bit of variability in answers for this question. The most frequently reported confidence of success was 100%. Fifty percent of the sample was 90% confident or higher. There is a very wide range of responses (96 percentage points), meaning that there are lots of differences in students' confidence ranging from 4% to 100%.

Again, this information would likely be used in the Participants section of the Method section of an APA-style paper, or in reporting the descriptive statistics of an outcome variable using the mean and the standard deviation like this:

The number of hours that participants reported that they spent in an average week studying, reading school related materials, and doing homework ranged from two to 25 hours ($M = 10.38$, $SD = 4.61$). On average, participants were 85.62% ($SD = 17.47\%$) confident that they would be successful in life.

## 2.4 Crosstabular Tables: Describing Categorical Data with Crosstabs

Because we can't calculate most descriptive statistics for categorical data, another way to look at categorical data is to describe the frequencies across two variables called a crosstabulation or a "crosstab" for short. This helps us see how many people are in a specific category of the first variable and who are also in a specific category for a second variable. For example, we could create a crosstab to see the frequency of students who use Twitter and who also use Facebook. Crosstabs help us describe our categorical data more richly by combining frequencies for two variables.

In our data for this chapter there are two categorical variables: personality trait (*trait*) and a question about whether or not students typically eat breakfast on weekdays (*breakfast*). We are going to see the frequencies of different personality traits and whether or not they eat breakfast by running a crosstab.

Select from the Top Menu Bar:

SPSS Commands
2.4

ANALYZE → DESCRIPTIVE STATISTICS → CROSSTABS

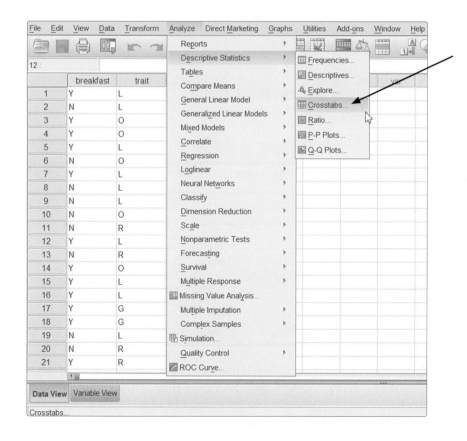

In the *Crosstabs* pop-up window, double-click *breakfast* from the left-hand side into the *Row(s)* box and *trait* from the left-hand side into the *Column(s)* box, then click **OK**. Note: It doesn't matter which of the two variables goes in the row or column, it is just personal preference.

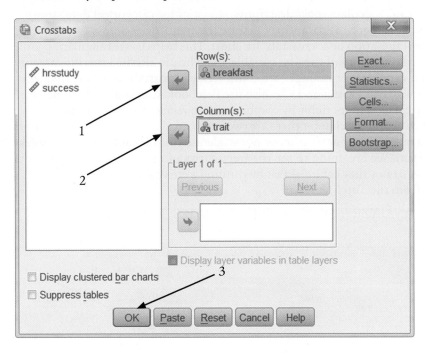

## breakfast * trait Crosstabulation

Count

| | | trait | | | | | | Total |
|---|---|---|---|---|---|---|---|---|
| | | Dark | Go-getter | Intellectual | Loving | Outgoing | Reserved | |
| breakfast | No | 0 | 0 | 2 | 8 | 7 | 5 | 22 |
| | Yes | 1 | 3 | 0 | 11 | 7 | 1 | 23 |
| Total | | 1 | 3 | 2 | 19 | 14 | 6 | 45 |

This crosstab shows us that of the students who report eating breakfast, 11 of them describe themselves as loving, followed by 7 describing themselves as outgoing. Of those students who describe themselves as outgoing (14 in all), half of them eat breakfast and half do not. This kind of crosstab gives us a way to describe how students respond on more than one categorical variable.

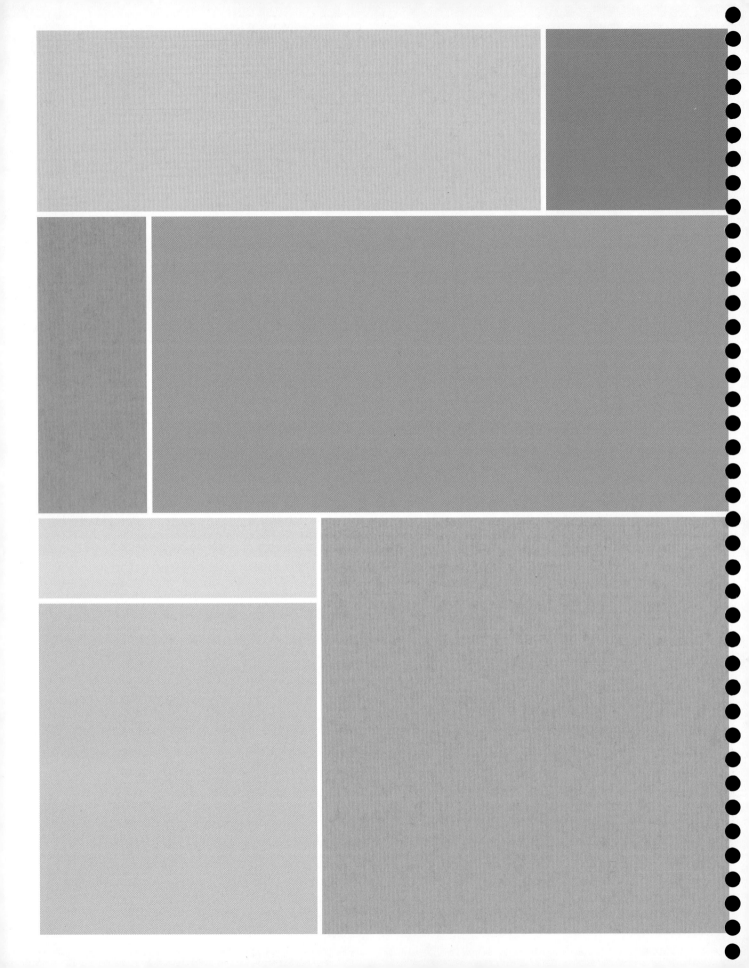

# Testing Association Claims

Research that is correlational means that the claims you are making are association claims. An association claim, like a causal claim, argues that levels of one variable are associated with or related to levels of another variable—as one variable changes, the other variable does as well. For example, we can make the claim that number of hours of studying is associated with exam performance—as hours of studying increase, exam scores also tend to increase. However, association claims are not causal claims because of the way the data are collected. In correlational studies that test association claims, the variables are measured, not manipulated or purposefully changed. Therefore, it is not possible to establish causation, because the variables are simply measured, not manipulated. For instance, when you give participants a survey one time, even though you measure many variables, you cannot make causal claims among them because you haven't manipulated any of those variables, nor do you have a time lag to say that one variable happened before another. For example, if we are interested in whether using flash cards is associated with exam scores and used a survey that asks students their exam score and whether or not they use flash

cards when studying, this is an association that we are testing. We didn't manipulate the flash card usage (i.e., randomly assigning half the class to use flash cards and the other half not to use flash cards) or plan for temporal precedence (i.e., have the students use flash cards before the first exam and then record their exam score afterwards), so we can't establish that using flash cards causes higher exam scores. We can only make the claim that using flash cards is positively associated with exam scores.

Depending on the type of data you have (e.g., quantitative or categorical), there are different methods to test association claims. When assessing association claims with quantitative variables, we describe the direction and the strength of the relationship between the variables using correlation. The direction describes either a positive or a negative association. In a positive association, both variables move in the same direction (i.e., as the first variable increases, the second variable also increases); for example, as salary increases, job satisfaction increases. In a negative association, the variables move in opposite directions (i.e., as the first variable increases, the second variable decreases); for example, as hours of sleep increase, irritability decreases. Of course, there can also be zero association where the relationship between the variables is nonexistent, in which case as the first variable increases, the second variable neither increases nor decreases. The strength refers to how close the association is to being perfectly linear, meaning that each time the first variable increases a specific amount, the second variable changes in a specific amount without variation from that pattern. For example, when salary increases, does job satisfaction increase consistently across all participants in a steady pattern? If yes, then the strength of that relationship would be strong, representing a consistent pattern of association. We refer to the strength of the correlation as an effect size, helping us determine if the effect is strong enough to be meaningful to our understanding of the relationship. Another way to consider strength is by testing to see if the relationship is statistically significant. In the next chapter, we will discover how to use IBM SPSS Statistics software ("SPSS") to compute a correlation value that allows us to see if that correlation is statistically significant, determining how likely the relationship is above chance alone. So, not only can we describe the strength of the relationship (effect size), we can also determine if it is statistically significant.

When assessing association claims between two categorical variables, we use basic crosstab tables and a statistic called chi-square. Because of the categorical nature of the data, direction cannot be assessed, only strength and statistical significance. In other words, we cannot say that as your hair color increases, your eye color increases, because the data are categorical. However, we can say that there is a strong relationship between what color hair and what color eyes a person has. In the next chapter, we will use SPSS to compute the chi-square statistic to test if there is a significant relationship between two categorical variables.

# 3

# Looking for Relationships
## Correlation, Reliability, and Chi-Square

*The correlation coefficient is one of the most common statistics out there to understand association claims. In this chapter, you will learn the fundamentals of interpreting associations using graphs, the application of the correlation for understanding relationships and reliability, and the use of chi-square for understanding relationships among categorical variables.*

## THE DATA

In this chapter, in addition to the five Likert-scale items that we recoded and summed in Chapter 1, we will use two more questions from that same data collected from the 45 students in my research methods class. We were interested in seeing if motivation was associated with academic success. A survey asked them the following questions:

1. **On a scale of 1 to 100 where 1 is *not at all* and 100 is *extremely*, how motivated are you to achieve?**

   _____

2. **What is your cumulative GPA to the nearest tenth (example: round 3.094 to 3.1)?** _____

Here's what these data look like in *Data View*, including the Likert-scale data we will use later in this chapter. We named the motivation item, *motscore*, and grade point average, *gpa*.

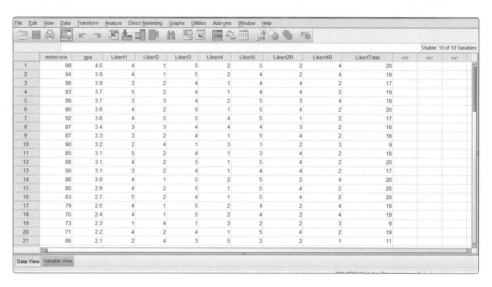

# Before We Get Started: Types of Variables and Association Claims

As we talked about in Chapter 1, there are two main types of data: quantitative (*Numeric*) data and categorical (*String*) data. The correlation coefficient is only a good statistic to use if you are testing the relationship between two variables and both variables are quantitative, numeric data. Testing the association between two variables is called bivariate correlation. A bivariate correlation can only measure a linear association. This means that as the first variable increases, the second variable must increase or decrease, but it must not increase first then decrease or change direction midway (called a *curvilinear association*). If your data are categorical, word-type data, then chi-square is the statistic that you should use to test bivariate association claims, as the correlation only works with quantitative variables. Keep in mind that association claims are just that, claiming that a relationship exists between the variables, but not that one variable causes the other. Causal claims need methods that manipulate a variable to test causation, and correlation is not an appropriate statistic to test such causal claims. (We will cover appropriate statistics for causal claims later in the book.)

# 3.1 Using Scatterplots to Show Association between Two Quantitative Variables

When we first take a look at our data, we want to get a general picture of what the relationship between the variables looks like. A scatterplot is an effective graphing technique to get a sense of the direction and strength of the relationship between the two quantitative variables.

In our example, we have two quantitative variables that we would like to graph to see their relationship: motivation to succeed (named *motscore*) and grade point average (named *gpa*). Our hypothesis is that higher motivation would be associated with higher GPA, so we are predicting a positive association. Here's how to get a scatterplot using SPSS to see if our hypothesis might be correct.

Select from the Top Menu Bar:

GRAPHS → CHART BUILDER

*SPSS Commands*
**3.1**

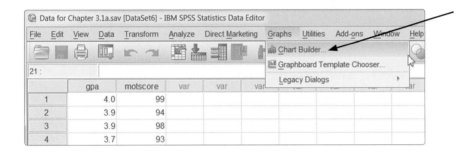

In the *Chart Builder* pop-up window, click **OK** as we have already defined our variables.

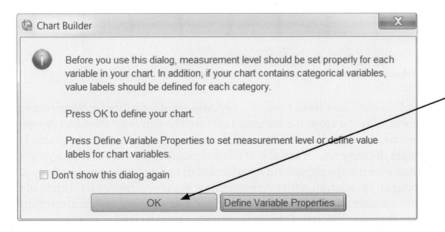

In the next *Chart Builder* pop-up window, under *Gallery*, choose *Scatter/Dot*, then choose *Simple Scatter* (the top left choice in the Gallery).

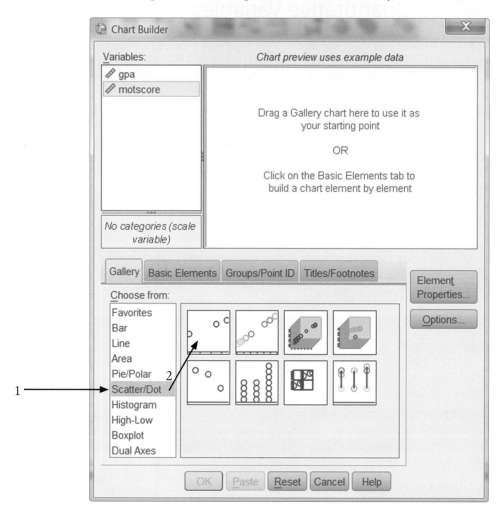

Next, while still in the *Chart Builder* pop-up window, on the top under *Variables* and the *Chart Preview*, drag *gpa* from the *Variables* box into the y-axis on the *Chart Preview* graph, and *motscore* from the *Variables* box into the x-axis on the *Chart Preview* graph. In this part, you are deciding which variable is the independent variable and dragging it to the x-axis and which is the dependent variable and dragging it to the y-axis. Because we are looking at an association, whichever variable goes on whichever axis is more of a choice. It doesn't matter what variable you put on the x-axis or y-axis when just testing an association. However, if you feel that one variable naturally leads to the other and that makes sense to you, then put that variable on the x-axis. For our example, it just made more sense to me to have motivation on the x-axis leading to GPA on the y-axis.

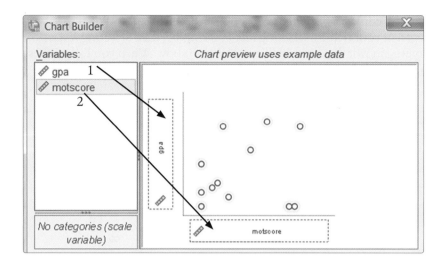

Then click on *Titles/Footnotes* tab and check the box for *Title 1* that shows up when you click the *Titles/Footnotes* tab. In the *Element Properties* pop-up window that shows to the right, type in your title under *Content* (e.g., "Scatterplot of Motivation Score with GPA"). After you type in the title, click **Apply** down at the bottom right, then click **OK**.

Like this:

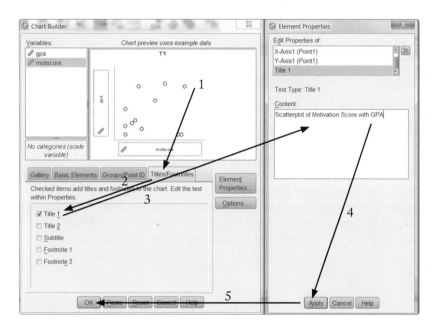

As a side note, you could also change the labels of the x-axis and y-axis right above where you typed in your title by selecting *Edit Properties of:*, then selecting *X-Axis1* or *Y-Axis1* and typing in what you would like the label to show. When you follow these instructions, SPSS will make a scatterplot like the graph shown below.

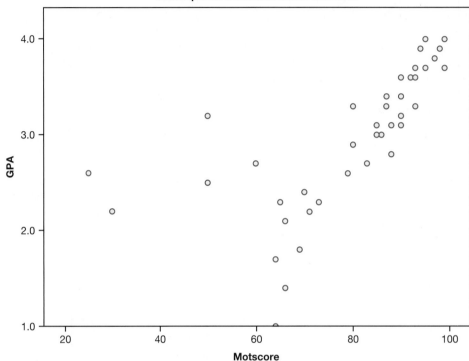

Scatterplot of Motivation Score with GPA

This scatterplot shows that motivation appears to be positively related to GPA. You can interpret the graph this way because you can see that the dots on the scatterplot seem to trend from lower left to upper right. As motivation increases, GPA generally increases. It is not a perfect relationship: GPA doesn't always increase when motivation does, but it generally follows that pattern. Although scatterplots are helpful to get an idea about the association between two variables and visualize it, there is a statistic that can be calculated that indicates the exact direction and strength of the relationship—namely, the Pearson correlation coefficient.

## 3.2 Using Bivariate Correlation to Show Association between Two Quantitative Variables

To accurately assess the direction and strength of the relationship between two variables, we will use the Pearson correlation coefficient (most often referred to simply as *correlation*). This statistic, whose symbol is *r*, will tell us the direction and strength of the relationship between our two variables (effect size), and this can be tested to see if that association is statistically significant. Here's how to run a bivariate (two variable) correlation.

Select from the Top Menu Bar:

ANALYZE → CORRELATE → BIVARIATE

*SPSS Commands*
*3.2*

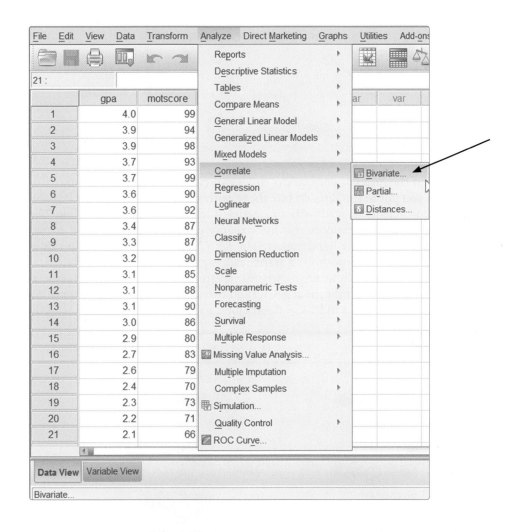

In the *Bivariate Correlations* pop-up window, double click *gpa* and *motscore* from the left-hand side into the *Variables* box, then click **OK** as everything is set by default.

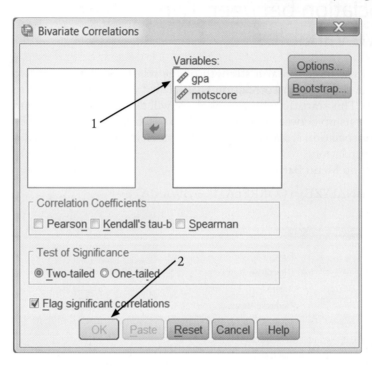

SPSS Output 3.2

When you run the *Bivariate* correlation, SPSS will give you a correlation matrix of the variables you put in the *Variables* box above, with statistically significant Pearson correlation coefficients flagged with an asterisk, such as in the output below. The same correlation is listed twice in this matrix: once in the upper right-hand corner and again in the lower left-hand corner. The *Sig. (2-tailed)* values are the *p* values that tell us if our correlation shows a statistically significant association. Statistical significance is also shown by asterisks, where one asterisk corresponds to an association that is statistically significant at $p < .05$ and two asterisks at $p < .01$. (Note: SPSS rounds to the nearest thousandths so the smallest *p* value that will be listed is .000.)

## Correlations

|  |  | gpa | motscore |
|---|---|---|---|
| gpa | Pearson Correlation | 1 | .684** |
|  | Sig. (2-tailed) |  | .000 |
|  | N | 45 | 45 |
| motscore | Pearson Correlation | .684** | 1 |
|  | Sig. (2-tailed) | .000 |  |
|  | N | 45 | 45 |

**Correlation is significant at the .01 level (2-tailed).

The Pearson correlation coefficient describes both the direction and the strength of the association between motivational score and GPA, as well as whether that association is strong enough to be considered statistically significant. SPSS gives you the correlation in matrix format, where the same information is shown twice, mirrored along the diagonal axis. The first line in the cell between *motscore* and *gpa* shows the Pearson correlation coefficient, which is .684 (highlighted in the SPSS output above). We can interpret that by saying there is a positive and strong association between motivation and GPA—as motivation increases, GPA generally increases as well. We know the relationship is positive because the correlation value is positive. We know it is strong by following the general conventions set out by Cohen (1988), specifying that correlations smaller than .3 are weak, between .3 and .6 are moderate, and larger than .6 are strong. Because .684 is larger than .6, we would describe the relationship as strong. We can also tell that the association between motivation and GPA is statistically significant. We know this because the $p$ value is less than .05, and any $p$ value less than .05 would be considered statistically significant. SPSS lists the $p$ value (in this case, $p$ = .000) and also flags this significant correlation with two asterisks that correspond to a $p$ value less than .01, shown at the bottom of the table.

APA Style 3.2

In order to report this result in APA style, we will need several pieces of information. First, the symbol for correlation is *r*. Second, we will need to calculate the degrees of freedom, which are calculated by the sample size (N on the output) minus two, so in this case, 60 – 2 = 58. Then, we will need the actual correlation value rounded to two places past the decimal point (.68). Finally, we will need the $p$ value rounded to two places past the decimal point that is listed under *Sig. (2-tailed)*. In our example, $p$ is so small that it rounds to .00, so it is convention to list that as less than .01, rather than the exact number .00. However, if the $p$ value were .027, for instance, then you would list $p$ = .03. This is what your APA-style Results section would look like for this finding:

We hypothesized that student motivation would be positively associated with grade point average (GPA). As hypothesized, motivation was significantly and positively related to GPA, $r(58)$ = .68, $p$ < .01.

## 3.3 Using Correlation to Test Reliability: Internal, Test-Retest, and Inter-Rater Reliability

Another use for measures of association like the correlation is to assess the reliability of your measure. Reliability refers to the consistency of your pattern of responses. There are three types of reliability. Internal reliability refers to how consistently a respondent answers multiple items assessing the same concept. For example, if we wanted to measure the concept of extroversion, rather than asking just one question, we may want to ask each participant several questions about extroversion, such as "I enjoy meeting new people," "I prefer to spend time by myself," and "I like to attend parties." We need to be sure that when we ask multiple items about the same concept, those items are answered consistently for each participant, and we assess that with internal reliability tests. Test-retest reliability refers to how consistent the measure is every time it is used. For example, we may give participants the same survey every month and be sure that participants answer those questions with consistency over time. Inter-rater reliability refers to how consistent the results are across multiple observers. For example, we may want to observe children playing in a daycare setting to record the amount of sharing behavior. When there is more than one observer coding the same child's behavior, observers' ratings should be consistent with each other. We call this inter-rater reliability.

### 3.3a   Internal Reliability

Often, when we measure a construct we use multiple items rather than just a single item. One of the important ways that we can determine if these multiple items are doing a good job in measuring the construct is to assess internal reliability. For this type of reliability, the best measure is Cronbach's alpha ($\alpha$), which is a correlation-based measure that computes the average of all the correlations of each item with all other items. Normally, a Cronbach's alpha of .7 or above is considered good internal reliability.

---

**THE DATA** ──────────────────────────────────────────

For this example, we will use the five Likert-scale items assessing opinions about the research methods class from Chapter 1 to illustrate computation of Cronbach's alpha. These five items were designed to measure the concept of positive opinions about the research methods class.

1. **The material we cover in this class is easy for me to understand.**

   Strongly Disagree          Disagree          Neutral          Agree          Strongly Agree

2. **There is a good chance that I will receive a low grade in this class.**

   Strongly Disagree          Disagree          Neutral          Agree          Strongly Agree

3. **I am confident that I will be successful in this class.**

   Strongly Disagree          Disagree          Neutral          Agree          Strongly Agree

4. **I am often confused after learning something new in this class.**

   Strongly Disagree          Disagree          Neutral          Agree          Strongly Agree

5. **I know my grade in this class will be higher than my classmates.**

   Strongly Disagree          Disagree          Neutral          Agree          Strongly Agree

---

We are trying to assess opinions about the research methods class using multiple items, and we would like to see whether a respondent answers consistently over the five items. Note that we will use the reverse coded items for *Likert2* and *Likert4* (see Chapter 1, Section 1.5, for details about reverse coding) to insure that a higher score indicates a more positive opinion for all five questions. If these five items consistently measure positive opinions about the research methods class, then a participant who answers *Agree* or *Strongly Agree* on *Likert1* would also answer *Agree* or *Strongly Agree* on *Likert3*.

To run Internal Reliability select from the Top Menu Bar:

*SPSS Commands*
**3.3a**

ANALYZE → SCALE → RELIABILITY ANALYSIS

| | Likert2 | Likert3 | | t2R | Likert4R | LikertTotal |
|---|---|---|---|---|---|---|
| 1 | 1 | 5 | | 2 | 4 | 20 |
| 2 | 1 | 5 | | 2 | 4 | 19 |
| 3 | 2 | 4 | | 4 | 2 | 17 |
| 4 | 2 | 4 | | 4 | 2 | 19 |
| 5 | 3 | 4 | | 3 | 4 | 19 |
| 6 | 2 | 5 | | 4 | 2 | 20 |
| 7 | 5 | 5 | | 1 | 2 | 17 |
| 8 | 3 | 4 | | 3 | 2 | 16 |
| 9 | 2 | 4 | | 4 | 2 | 18 |
| 10 | 4 | 1 | | 2 | 3 | 9 |
| 11 | 2 | 4 | | | | |
| 12 | 2 | 5 | | | | |
| 13 | 2 | 4 | | | | |
| 14 | 1 | 5 | | | | |
| 15 | 2 | 5 | | 4 | 2 | 20 |
| 16 | 2 | 4 | | 4 | 2 | 20 |
| 17 | 1 | 5 | | 2 | 4 | 19 |
| 18 | 1 | 5 | | 2 | 4 | 19 |
| 19 | 4 | 1 | | 2 | 3 | 9 |
| 20 | 2 | 4 | | 4 | 2 | 19 |
| 21 | 4 | 3 | | 2 | 1 | 11 |

Analyze menu items:
Reports
Descriptive Statistics
Tables
Compare Means
General Linear Model
Generalized Linear Models
Mixed Models
Correlate
Regression
Loglinear
Neural Networks
Classify
Dimension Reduction
Scale → Reliability Analysis...
Nonparametric Tests → Multidimensional Unfolding (PREFSCAL)...
Forecasting → Multidimensional Scaling (PROXSCAL)...
Survival → Multidimensional Scaling (ALSCAL)...
Multiple Response
Missing Value Analysis...
Multiple Imputation
Complex Samples
Simulation...
Quality Control
ROC Curve...

Data View   Variable View

Reliability Analysis...

In the *Reliability Analysis* pop-up window, double click the items you would like to be analyzed from the variable list on the left into the *Items:* window on the right. For our example, the three original Likert-scale original items and the two reverse-coded Likert-scale items were selected into the *Items:* window. The default is already set for the *Model: Alpha*, which is Cronbach's alpha, so go ahead and click **OK**.

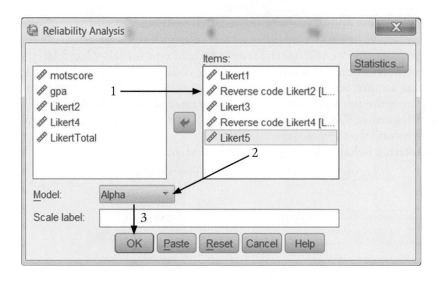

*SPSS Output*
**3.3a**

When you run this analysis, SPSS produces the following reliability output.

## Reliability

---

### Scale: ALL VARIABLES

---

**Case Processing Summary**

| | | N | % |
|---|---|---|---|
| Cases | Valid | 45 | 100.0 |
| | Excludedᵃ | 0 | .0 |
| | Total | 45 | 100.0 |

a. Listwise deletion based on all variables in the procedure.

**Reliability Statistics**

| Cronbach's Alpha | N of Items |
|---|---|
| .757 | 5 |

*Interpretation*
**3.3a**

In the table labeled *Reliability Statistics*, under Cronbach's alpha (whose symbol is α), you will see that the reliability is .757 (highlighted in the table) for the five items. (See *N of items* to verify how many items were used in the Cronbach's alpha calculation.) Using Cohen's (1988) conventions, we would consider these five items to have acceptable internal reliability because Cronbach's alpha is greater than .70.

You would likely report the reliability of a scale in the Materials section of the Method section of an APA-style paper. Here is an example of how you might report Cronbach's alpha:

> Participants rated five, 5-point Likert-scale items about their opinions of the research methods class (e.g., "The material we cover in this class is easy for me to understand"). Response categories ranged from *Strongly Disagree* to *Strongly Agree*. We added these five statements together to create a summed total opinion score ($\alpha = .76$).

## 3.3b  Test-Retest Reliability

Test-retest reliability refers to how consistent a measure is over time. Assessing test-retest reliability makes sense if what you are measuring is thought to be stable over time. For example, we might want to test if student responses to the 5-item opinion survey about the research methods class remain stable over time. To test this, we would correlate responses to the summed score (*LikertTotal*) at time 1 with the summed score at a time 2, expecting that those scores would be highly correlated [$r > .7$ using Cohen's (1988) conventions]. To conduct this test-retest reliability analysis, you would follow the instructions for bivariate correlation in Section 3.2 in this chapter, using *LikertTotal* at time 1 and *LikertTotal* at time 2 as the two variables in your test.

## 3.3c  Inter-Rater Reliability

Inter-rater reliability measures consistency across multiple observers or raters. Assessing inter-rater reliability makes sense if you have more than one observer collecting data and you want to be sure that the measurement is consistent among those multiple observers. In the example below, we had two observers count how many times during a 5-minute speech their fellow classmates said the word "uhm." We would expect that the number that the first observer reports would be similar to the number the other observer reports, resulting in good inter-rater reliability. Like test-retest reliability, if your observations are quantitative, you can use the correlation to assess inter-rater reliability. Using Cohen's (1988) criteria, a correlation greater than .7 would be considered reliable. (See bivariate correlation in Section 3.2 in this chapter for how to run the correlation using the first rater's values as the first variable and the second rater's values as the second variable.)

If your variables are categorical, then another statistic should be used to assess inter-rater agreement. The Kappa statistic is a measure of the degree and significance of agreement between raters. The Kappa statistic has values much like a correlation with a maximum of 1.0 and a minimum of 0, with a value of .7 and above considered acceptable inter-rater reliability.

For this example, we are using data from two raters who were rating levels of use of the word "uhm" during a 5-minute speech. The raters gave a 1 for low level, 2 for moderate level, and 3 for high level use of the word "uhm."

The data were entered for all of the 25 students evaluated by each observer. Data were entered in two columns, where the first rater's categorization of level are called *Rater1Obs*, and the second raters categorization of level are called *Rater2Obs*, like this:

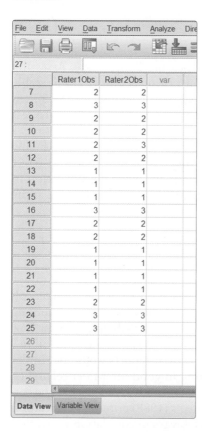

To have SPSS compute a Kappa statistic, select from the Top Menu Bar:

ANALYZE → DESCRIPTIVE STATISTICS → CROSSTABS

SPSS Commands
3.3c

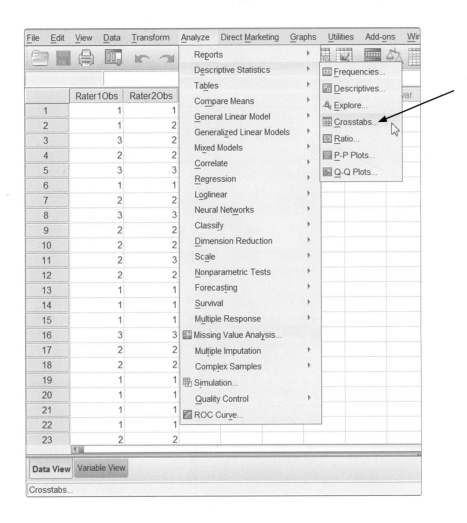

In the *Crosstabs* pop-up window, highlight *Rater1Obs* and click on the arrow pointing to the *Rows* box, and then highlight *Rater2Obs* and click on the arrow pointing to the *Columns* box, then select the [Statistics ...] button.

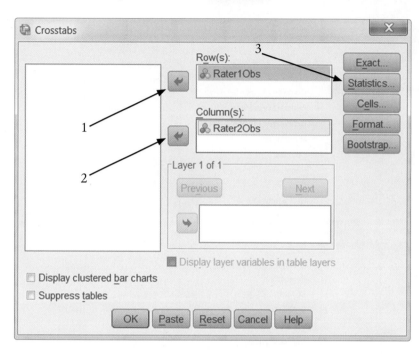

In the *Statistics* pop-up window, select only *Kappa*, then click [Continue], then click [OK].

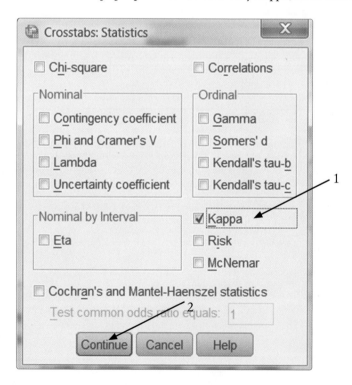

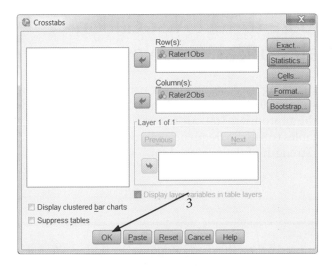

When you run the Crosstabs command and specify the Kappa statistic, this is the table SPSS gives you for Kappa:

SPSS Output
3.3c

## Symmetric Measures

| | | Value | Asymp. Std. Error[a] | Approx. T[b] | Approx. Sig. |
|---|---|---|---|---|---|
| Measure of Agreement | Kappa | .817 | .099 | 5.716 | .000 |
| N of Valid Cases | | 25 | | | |

a. Not assuming the null hypothesis.
b. Using the asymptotic standard error assuming the null hypothesis.

The value for the Kappa statistic highlighted in the table above is .817, showing that rater 1 and rater 2 have acceptable agreement (>.7), and that their agreement is statistically significant because the $p$ value (*Approx. Sig.*) is less than .05 ($p < .001$).

Interpretation
3.3c

APA Style
3.3c

You would likely write about inter-rater reliability in the Method section of an APA-style paper like this:

> To establish inter-rater reliability, two raters observed each of the 25 participants and categorized the number of times they said the word "uhm" into three categories: low, moderate, and high. The raters showed acceptable and statistically significant agreement, *Kappa* = .82, $p < .001$.

# 3.4 Using Chi-Square to Test Association Claims for Two Categorical Variables

When our data are categorical, testing association claims using the Pearson correlation ($r$) won't work because correlation is only used for quantitative data. For categorical data, chi-square is the appropriate statistic to test the significance of the relationship. We use crosstab tables to see the frequencies across two variables, and then use chi-square to test the strength of their association.

---

**THE DATA**

---

In the data from Chapter 2 there were two questions, listed below, that had categorical responses. We will use these questions for the chi-square test to see if there is a significant association between personality trait (this variable is named *trait*) and whether the person typically eats breakfast on weekdays (this variable is named *breakfast*). In other words, we wanted to see if breakfast-eaters are more likely to describe themselves with a certain personality trait compared to other traits. We hypothesized that outgoing and loving people would be more likely to eat breakfast.

1. **Do you typically eat breakfast on weekdays?**

   YES                    NO

2. **The personality trait that best describes me is (please circle only one):**

   Outgoing        Go-getter        Dark        Loving        Reserved        Intellectual

---

*SPSS Commands*
**3.4**

Select from the Top Menu Bar:

ANALYZE → DESCRIPTIVE STATISTICS → CROSSTABS

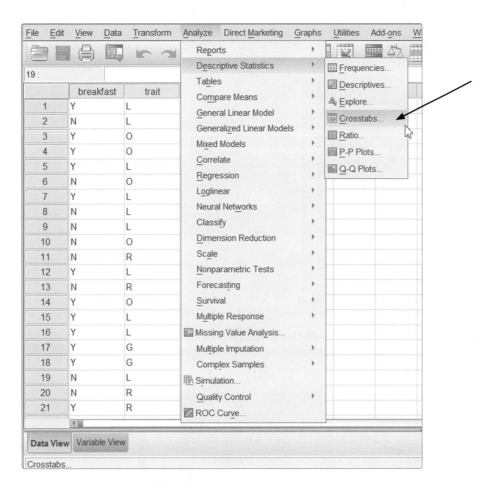

In the *Crosstabs* pop-up window, highlight *breakfast* from the left-hand side and click the arrow pointing to the *Row(s)* box, and highlight *trait* from the left-hand side and click the arrow pointing to the *Column(s)* box, then click the **Statistics...** button.

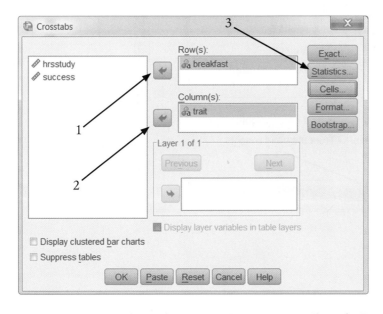

In the *Crosstabs: Statistics* pop-up window, select *Chi-square* and *Phi and Cramer's V*, then click Continue . We will use the chi-square for our significance test and phi for reporting the effect size of that chi-square.

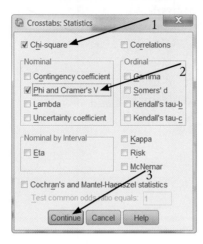

Then, in the *Crosstabs* window, click the Cells... button. In the *Crosstabs: Cells* pop-up window, select Observed Counts and Row and Column Percentages, then click Continue , then click OK .

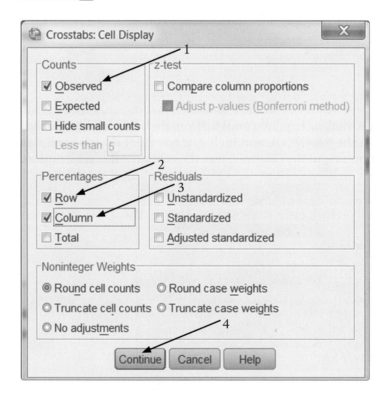

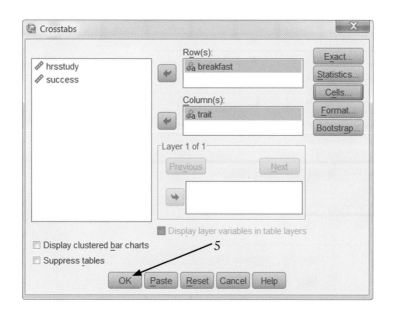

Here are the four tables of output that SPSS provides for the chi-square analysis.

SPSS Output
3.4

## Case Processing Summary

| | Cases | | | | | |
|---|---|---|---|---|---|---|
| | Valid | | Missing | | Total | |
| | N | Percent | N | Percent | N | Percent |
| breakfast * trait | 45 | 100.0% | 0 | 0.0% | 45 | 100.0% |

## breakfast * trait Crosstabulation

| | | | trait | | | | | | Total |
|---|---|---|---|---|---|---|---|---|---|
| | | | Dark | Go-getter | Intellectual | Loving | Outgoing | Reserved | |
| breakfast | No | Count | 0 | 0 | 2 | 8 | 7 | 5 | 22 |
| | | % within breakfast | 0.0% | 0.0% | 9.1% | 36.4% | 31.8% | 22.7% | 100.0% |
| | | % within trait | 0.0% | 0.0% | 100.0% | 42.1% | 50.0% | 83.3% | 48.9% |
| | Yes | Count | 1 | 3 | 0 | 11 | 7 | 1 | 23 |
| | | % within breakfast | 4.3% | 13.0% | 0.0% | 47.8% | 30.4% | 4.3% | 100.0% |
| | | % within trait | 100.0% | 100.0% | 0.0% | 57.9% | 50.0% | 16.7% | 51.1% |
| Total | | Count | 1 | 3 | 2 | 19 | 14 | 6 | 45 |
| | | % within breakfast | 2.2% | 6.7% | 4.4% | 42.2% | 31.1% | 13.3% | 100.0% |
| | | % within trait | 100.0% | 100.0% | 100.0% | 100.0% | 100.0% | 100.0% | 100.0% |

## Chi-Square Tests

| | Value | df | Asymp. Sig. (2-sided) |
|---|---|---|---|
| Pearson Chi-Square | 9.123a | 5 | .104 |
| Likelihood Ratio | 11.682 | 5 | .039 |
| N of Valid Cases | 45 | | |

a. 8 cells (66.7%) have expected count less than 5. The minimum expected count is .49.

## Symmetric Measures

| | | Value | Approx. Sig. |
|---|---|---|---|
| Nominal by Nominal | Phi | .450 | .104 |
| | Cramer's V | .450 | .104 |
| N of Valid Cases | | 45 | |

*Interpretation 3.4*

For the chi-square analysis, the first table (*Case Processing Summary*) tells us how many people completed data for both variables. The second table (*breakfast * trait Crosstabulation*) is the crosstab showing the frequency and the percentage of people who belong to a specific category for *breakfast* and for *trait*.

The chi-square statistic, whose symbol is $\chi^2$, is found in the third table (*Chi-Square Tests*), in the row titled Pearson Chi-Square (highlighted above). The *Asymp. Sig. (2-sided)* p value that is above .05 tells us there is not a statistically significant relationship between whether a person typically eats breakfast and their personality type. This finding is further supported by the Phi statistic ($\varphi$), found in the *Symmetric Measures* table (highlighted above), where the p value (*Approx. Sig.*) is also above .05, and therefore not significant. We will use this Phi statistic as a measure of effect size when reporting in APA style as well.

It is also important to note from the warning between Tables 3 and 4 (highlighted above), that there are eight cells with an expected count less than five. An assumption of the chi-square test is that all cells will have an expected count of five or greater in order for the results to be reliable, and unfortunately these data do not meet this assumption. When your data fail to meet the assumptions of the statistical test you are running, there are several options you can choose to pursue. You can just take the results with a grain a salt and report the limitation in the write-up of your results, or you can try to find another statistical test that better suits your data (see Chapter 7 for some options).

There are several pieces of information we will need in order to write up these results in APA style. First, we will need the chi-square value, the degrees of freedom (*df*), the *p* value [*Asymp. Sig. (2-sided)*], and the phi (φ) value. Here is what this result might look like in APA style, noting that the finding is not significant:

> We hypothesized that there would be a significant relationship between self-reported personality trait and whether or not a person typically eats breakfast with more outgoing and loving people being more likely to eat breakfast. This hypothesis was not supported, $\chi^2(5, N = 45) = 9.12$, *ns*, φ = .45.

APA Style
3.4

### Reference

Cohen, J. (1988). *Statistical power analysis for the behavioral sciences*, 2nd ed. Hillsdale, NJ: Erlbaum.

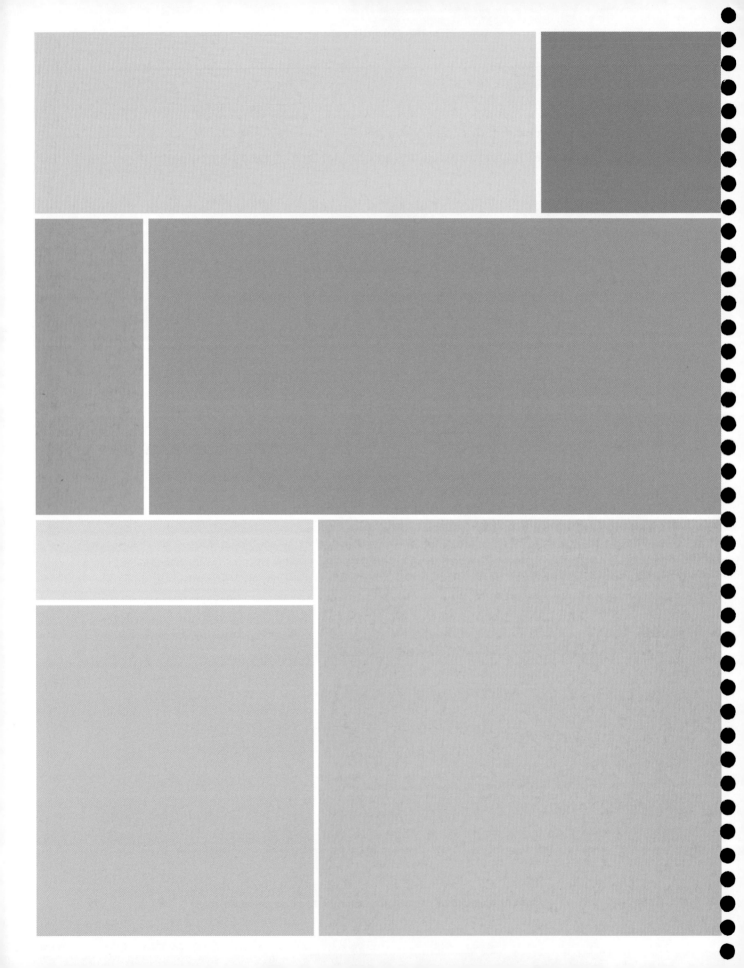

# Making Causal Claims

In the previous chapter, we have been discovering how to test association claims answering questions like, "Is there a significant relationship between motivation and GPA?" However, association claims are not as powerful as causal claims that would answer questions like, "Does having a tattoo cause a person to be perceived as less intelligent?" Causal claims are certainly more powerful, but they must be made only when the research methodology is sound and the statistical analysis is appropriate to make claims of causation. Experimental designs are used to collect data that we can test for causation. Experimentation is a method of collecting data where a variable is manipulated by the researcher, and then its effect on another variable is measured. An example of this is when a researcher gives one randomly assigned group of participants a picture of a person without a tattoo, and another randomly assigned group of participants that same picture with a tattoo photo-shopped onto the person's arm, and then measures both groups' perceptions of

that person's intelligence. We call the variable that we manipulate, the independent variable (or the factor), and the variable that we expect to show an effect, the dependent variable. In the example, the independent variable is the tattoo condition (with two levels: presence or absence of a tattoo), and the dependent variable is the intelligence rating.

Much of the responsibility for making sure that causation is an appropriate claim lies in the research methodology used. The researcher must insure that the research method meets three criteria in order to make a causal claim: (1) the variables must be associated, (2) the independent variable must have temporal precedence to (come before) the dependent variable, and (3) internal validity must be established, ruling out other variables that might account for the association. The next two chapters will explain how to statistically test for different types of causal claims, but remember that causal claims should only be made if the method used to collect the data meets the three criteria above.

# 4

# Simple Experiments
## Testing Simple Differences in Means

*Comparing sample means is one of the most common statistical procedures used when a researcher employs an experimental design to test a hypothesis. This chapter will cover the independent-samples t test that compares two sample means to test for a significant difference, one-way analysis of variance that compares two or more sample means to test for significant differences, and the paired-samples t test that compares two sample means that are paired in some way to test for a significant difference.*

The data we will use for this chapter comes from a research project conducted in my research methods class in three phases. The researchers were interested in intelligence ratings of people in photographs. In the first phase of the study, the researchers were interested in whether tattoos impacted perception of intelligence of the pictured Woman 1. In the second phase of the study (see Section 4.2), researchers were interested in perceptions of intelligence of Woman 1 without tattoos after the participants were supplied with information about her education level. In Section 4.3, we will look at the third phase, in which participants saw both Woman 1 and Woman 2 without tattoos, but dressed more casually or professionally, and rated their intelligence based on the attire.

For the first phase of the study, participants were randomly assigned to two groups and shown two photographs of women (one at a time): the first group seeing both women without tattoos (shown below on the left), and the second group seeing the first woman with a tattoo and the second woman without a tattoo (shown below on the right). The independent variable is tattoo condition because the researchers manipulated it. There are two levels of the tattoo condition: no tattoo versus a tattoo on her arm. Students were instructed to rate each woman's intelligence on a scale of 1 (*not at all intelligent*) to 10 (*extremely intelligent*). This rating is the dependent variable. Participants also indicated whether or not they had a tattoo themselves. Here is what the experiment looked like:

**Woman 1 and Woman 2 without tattoo**      **Woman 1 with tattoo, Woman 2 without tattoo**

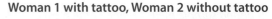

Please write your response on the line below each picture, rating the intelligence of each person in the photograph on a scale of 1 to 10 (where 1 is *not at all intelligent* and 10 is *extremely intelligent*). Note: Participants saw each picture separately.

Do you have one or more tattoos on your body?                    YES            NO

When entering this data into SPSS, the first variable entered was the group that the student belonged to, which I named *Group* with 1 being the *no tattoo* group and 2 being the *tattoo* group. Second, we entered the answer to the question about whether the participant had a tattoo, named *HaveTattoo* as 1 (*don't have a tattoo*) and 2 (*have a tattoo*). Finally, we entered in their intelligence ratings for Woman 1 (named *IntelligenceW1*) and Woman 2 (named *IntelligenceW2*). This is what the data look like in *Data View* in SPSS.

| File | Edit | View | Data | Transform | Analyze | Direct Marketing | Graphs |
|------|------|------|------|-----------|---------|-----------------|--------|

|   | Group | HaveTattoo | IntelligentW1 | IntelligentW2 | var |
|---|-------|-----------|---------------|---------------|-----|
| 1 | 1 | 1 | 7 | 8 | |
| 2 | 1 | 2 | 6 | 6 | |
| 3 | 1 | 2 | 9 | 8 | |
| 4 | 1 | 2 | 7 | 8 | |
| 5 | 1 | 1 | 5 | 6 | |
| 6 | 1 | 1 | 8 | 7 | |
| 7 | 1 | 2 | 7 | 7 | |
| 8 | 1 | 1 | 6 | 7 | |
| 9 | 1 | 2 | 6 | 8 | |
| 10 | 1 | 1 | 7 | 7 | |
| 11 | 1 | 2 | 8 | 8 | |
| 12 | 1 | 2 | 5 | 6 | |
| 13 | 1 | 2 | 7 | 9 | |
| 14 | 1 | 1 | 7 | 8 | |
| 15 | 1 | 1 | 6 | 8 | |
| 16 | 1 | 1 | 6 | 7 | |
| 17 | 1 | 1 | 5 | 7 | |
| 18 | 1 | 1 | 8 | 10 | |
| 19 | 1 | 2 | 9 | 9 | |
| 20 | 1 | 1 | 10 | 10 | |
| 21 | 1 | 1 | 6 | 8 | |

Data View    Variable View

# Before We Get Started: Between-Groups versus Within-Groups Designs

When testing causal claims from experimental designs, there are two main ways to expose participants to the independent variable that has been manipulated. Researchers can randomly assign participants to two independent groups and then expose one group to one level of the independent variable and the other group to the other level of the independent variable. This would be what we call a *between-groups design* (also called *independent-groups design*). In the example for this chapter, the between-group design is between the group who saw Woman 1 without the tattoo and the group who saw Woman 1 with the tattoo. A second way to expose participants to the different levels of the independent variable is to expose the same participants to both levels of the independent variable, which is called a *within-groups design*. In the example for this chapter, the within-group design is that both groups were exposed to both women's pictures to compare their own rating of Woman 1 to Woman 2. These two designs require different statistical analyses, depending on whether the same participants were exposed to both levels of the independent variable (Woman 1 and Woman 2), or the participants were assigned to two groups and each group was exposed to a different level of the independent variable (Woman 1 without tattoo and Woman 1 with tattoo).

## 4.1 Testing Between-Group Experimental Differences: Independent-Samples *T* Tests

When participants are randomly assigned to groups that receive different levels of an independent variable, this is called a *between-groups experiment*. In our particular example for this chapter, we will statistically test for differences between the two samples (Woman 1 with tattoo versus Woman 1 without tattoo) using an independent-samples *t* test. The independent variable is categorical, exposing each sample to a different level of the variable, and the dependent variable is quantitative, which allows us to calculate and compare means. In our example, the independent variable that was manipulated in the between-groups design was whether or not Woman 1 had a tattoo. Students were randomly assigned to see either the picture of Woman 1 without a tattoo or with a tattoo on her arm. The dependent variable was a quantitative measure of her intelligence, rated on a scale of 1 to 10. For this between-groups design, we will not be including their ratings of Woman 2. Here is how we would test to see if there is a significant difference in mean intelligence ratings for the group who saw Woman 1 with a tattoo compared to the group who saw her without a tattoo.

*SPSS Commands 4.1*

Select from the Top Menu Bar:

ANALYZE → COMPARE MEANS → INDEPENDENT-SAMPLES T TEST

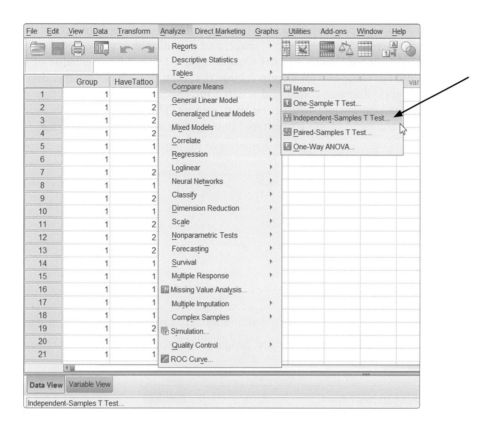

In the *Independent-Samples T Test* pop-up window, highlight your dependent variable and click the arrow pointing to the *Test Variable(s)* window like in the example with *IntelligentW1*, then highlight your independent variable and click the arrow pointing to the *Grouping Variable:* window like in the example with *Group*, then click the *Define Groups* button.

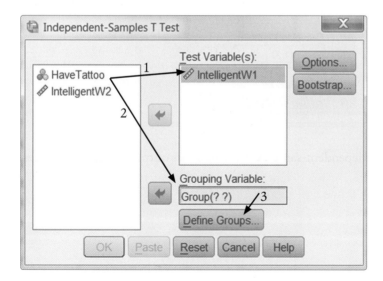

In the *Define Groups* pop-up window, put the value that you entered into the data spreadsheet for Group 1 in the *Group 1:* space, and the value that you entered into the data spreadsheet for Group 2 in the *Group 2:* space. I entered in the value of 1 for Group 1 and the value of 2 for Group 2. Note that even though the independent variable is categorical, it was coded and entered into SPSS as a number, so that a number is entered here when you define your groups. The values you enter here must be exactly the same values you entered in your data set. Then click Continue .

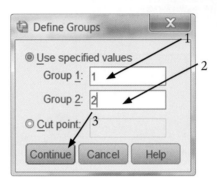

That will take you back to the *Independent-Samples T Test* pop-up window, where you can click OK .

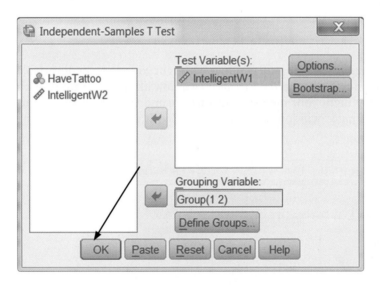

SPSS Output
4.1
When you run this Independent-samples *t* test, this is the output that SPSS provides.

## T Test

### Group Statistics

| | Group | N | Mean | Std. Deviation | Std. Error Mean |
|---|---|---|---|---|---|
| IntelligentW1 | No Tattoos | 25 | 6.92 | 1.288 | .258 |
| | Tattoos | 25 | 6.00 | 1.581 | .316 |

### Independent Samples Test

| | | Levene's Test for Equality of Variances | | T Test for Equality of Means | | | | | 95% Confidence Interval of the Difference | |
|---|---|---|---|---|---|---|---|---|---|---|
| | | F | Sig. | t | df | Sig. (2-tailed) | Mean Difference | Std. Error Difference | Lower | Upper |
| Intelligent W1 | Equal variances assumed | 1.581 | .215 | 2.255 | 48 | .029 | .920 | .408 | .100 | 1.740 |
| | Equal variances not assumed | | | 2.255 | 46.120 | .029 | .920 | .408 | .099 | 1.741 |

*Interpretation* **4.1**

In the first table called *Group Statistics*, SPSS provides standard descriptive statistics for the dependent variable for each group separately. For this data, we can see that the 25 participants in Group 1 who saw Woman 1 without the tattoo rated her intelligence on average at 6.92 out of a possible 10, plus or minus the standard deviation of 1.29 (highlighted in the *Group Statistics* table). The 25 participants in Group 2, who saw the same woman with the tattoo, rated her intelligence on average at 6.0, plus or minus the standard deviation of 1.58. So, we can see that the average intelligence rating was higher when the woman did not have a tattoo versus when she did have a tattoo. Furthermore, we can see that this difference was significant. In the *Independent Samples Test* table, we can see that the $t$ value, the degrees of freedom, and the $p$ value [called *Sig. (2-tailed)*] show there is a significant difference in the means because the $p$ value = .029, which is less than .05. This tells us that mean intelligence rating was significantly higher when the woman did not have a tattoo compared to when she did have a tattoo.

It is also important to note that SPSS checks to make sure that the assumption of equal population variances is met by the *Levene's Test for Equality of Variances* in the *Independent Samples Test* table highlighted above. For the *Independent Samples Test*, we assume that our two groups come from populations that are equivalent in their distribution, and the Levene's test tells us if this assumption has been violated.

If the *p* value (*Sig.*) for the Levene's test is less than .05, then our data violate the equality of variances assumption. When the assumption has been violated, we use the information for the *t* test from the line in the table labeled *Equal variances not assumed*. Otherwise, always use the *Equal variances assumed* statistics. The best case scenario is that the Levene's test is not significant (i.e., *p* > .05) so that we meet the assumption and can use the *Equal variances assumed* statistics. For the example data, the *p* value for the Levene's test was .215, which is greater than .05, so we can be confident that the assumption of equal population variances has been met, and we can use the *Equal variances assumed* statistics for this test.

*APA Style*
**4.1**

In order to report this test using APA style, we will need the means and standard deviations for both groups, as well as the *t* value, degrees of freedom, and *p* value (under *Sig. 2-tailed*). In addition, we will need to calculate a measure of effect size called *Cohen's d*. This is a statistic that needs to be hand-calculated using the following formula:

$$d = t\sqrt{\frac{N_1 + N_2}{N_1 N_2}}$$

For this problem, the calculations for *d* are:

$$d = 2.255\sqrt{\frac{25 + 25}{25 * 25}} = .64$$

So, your APA-style Results paragraph should look like this:

> We hypothesized that there would be a significant difference in rating of intelligence (on a scale from 1 to 10) for the woman in the first photograph for the group who saw her with a tattoo on her arm compared to the group who saw her without a tattoo. As predicted, rating of intelligence was significantly lower on average for the group who saw her with a tattoo (*M* = 6.00, *SD* = 1.58) compared to those who saw her without a tattoo (*M* = 6.92, *SD* = 1.29), *t*(48) = 2.26, *p* = .03, *d* = .64.

## 4.2 Testing Between-Group Experimental Differences: One-Way ANOVA

In some experiments, participants are randomly assigned to more than two independent groups. In this case, the *t* test is not appropriate, and so an analysis of variance (ANOVA) should be used. One-way ANOVA is a more powerful analysis that can test for differences between two or more sample means, not just two sample means.

**THE DATA**

In a second phase of the experiment used in Section 4.1, researchers were interested in using the picture of Woman 1 without the tattoo and adding another variable—her education level. Researchers randomly assigned participants to one of three groups based on Woman 1's education level: Group 1 read that she had graduated with a high school degree (see example below), Group 2 read that she had graduated with a college degree, and Group 3 read that she had graduated with a master's degree. The dependent variable in this phase of the experiment was the intelligence rating of Woman 1. The researchers hypothesized that Woman 1's intelligence rating would be significantly different among the three education levels, with the high school degree level being the lowest.

**This is Carmen. She has graduated with a high school degree.**

Please write your response on the line below the picture, rating the intelligence of the person in the photograph on a scale of 1 to 10 (where 1 is *not at all intelligent* and 10 is *extremely intelligent*). Note: Participants saw the picture separately.

The independent variable named *Education* has three levels, showing Woman 1 with information that she had graduated with a high school degree, college degree, or master's degree. The rating of intelligence is called *IntelligenceW1*. Here is what this data look like in *Data View*. Because there are more than two levels of the independent variable (in this case there are three levels), we must use a one-way ANOVA rather than an independent-samples *t* test.

| | Group | Education | HaveTattoo | IntelligentW 1 | IntelligentW 2 |
|---|---|---|---|---|---|
| 1 | 1 | 2 | 1 | 7 | 8 |
| 2 | 1 | 1 | 2 | 6 | 6 |
| 3 | 1 | 3 | 2 | 9 | 8 |
| 4 | 1 | 2 | 2 | 7 | 8 |
| 5 | 1 | 1 | 1 | 5 | 6 |
| 6 | 1 | 2 | 1 | 8 | 7 |
| 7 | 1 | 2 | 2 | 7 | 7 |
| 8 | 1 | 1 | 1 | 6 | 7 |
| 9 | 1 | 1 | 2 | 6 | 8 |
| 10 | 1 | 2 | 1 | 7 | 7 |
| 11 | 1 | 2 | 2 | 8 | 8 |
| 12 | 1 | 1 | 2 | 5 | 6 |
| 13 | 1 | 2 | 2 | 7 | 9 |
| 14 | 1 | 2 | 1 | 7 | 8 |
| 15 | 1 | 1 | 1 | 6 | 8 |
| 16 | 1 | 1 | 1 | 6 | 7 |
| 17 | 1 | 1 | 1 | 5 | 7 |
| 18 | 1 | 2 | 1 | 8 | 10 |
| 19 | 1 | 3 | 2 | 9 | 9 |
| 20 | 1 | 3 | 1 | 10 | 10 |
| 21 | 1 | 1 | 1 | 6 | 8 |

Data View | Variable View

In this example, the independent variable that was manipulated was whether Woman 1 had a high school, college, or master's degree, and the dependent variable was a quantitative measure of her intelligence, rated on a scale of 1 to 10. Here is how we would test to see if there is a significant difference in mean intelligence ratings among the groups using one-way ANOVA.

Select from the Top Menu Bar:

*SPSS Commands*
**4.2**

ANALYZE → COMPARE MEANS → ONE-WAY ANOVA

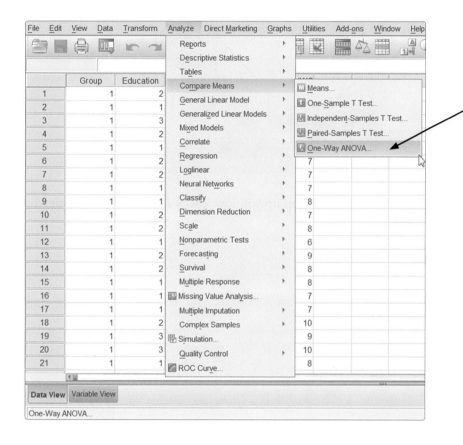

In the *One-Way ANOVA* pop-up window, highlight *IntelligentW1* and click the arrow pointing to the *Dependent List* box, and highlight *Education* and click the arrow pointing to the *Factor* box, then click **Options…**.

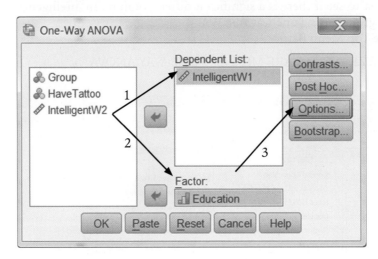

In the *One-Way ANOVA: Options* pop-up window, check *Descriptive* and *Means plot*, then click **Continue**.

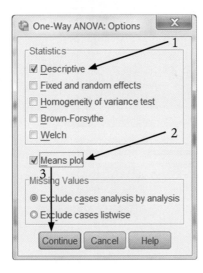

In the *One-Way ANOVA* pop-up window, again, click the [Post Hoc…] button.

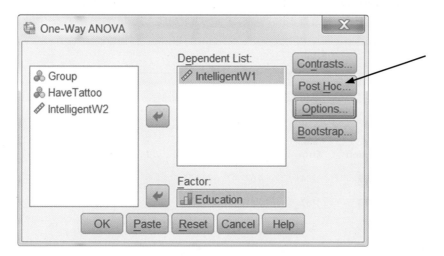

In the *One-Way ANOVA: Post Hoc Multiple Comparisons* pop-up window, choose one of the tests listed. There are many choices of *post hoc tests* that test differences between each level of the independent variable with each of the other levels. For instance, a post hoc test will compare the high school level mean with the college level mean, and then the master's level mean, and so on. The post hoc test choices listed on SPSS are similar to each other—with LSD, Bonferroni, Scheffe, and Tukey tests being the most commonly used in the social sciences. You can either choose one or select more than one, and decide which one to report later. I used *LSD* as my preferred choice. You would check *LSD*, then click [Continue], then click [OK].

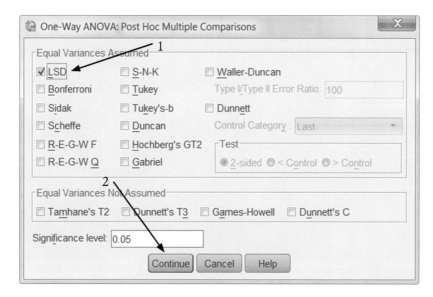

When you run this one-way ANOVA, these are the output tables SPSS provides.

## One Way

### Descriptives

**IntelligentW1**

| | N | Mean | Std. Deviation | Std. Error | 95% Confidence Interval for Mean Lower Bound | 95% Confidence Interval for Mean Upper Bound | Minimum | Maximum |
|---|---|---|---|---|---|---|---|---|
| High School grad | 20 | 5.10 | .912 | .204 | 4.67 | 5.53 | 3 | 6 |
| College grad | 22 | 6.95 | .785 | .167 | 6.61 | 7.30 | 5 | 8 |
| Master's grad | 8 | 8.50 | .926 | .327 | 7.73 | 9.27 | 7 | 10 |
| Total | 50 | 6.46 | 1.501 | .212 | 6.03 | 6.89 | 3 | 10 |

### ANOVA

**IntelligentW1**

| | Sum of Squares | df | Mean Square | F | Sig. |
|---|---|---|---|---|---|
| Between Groups | 75.665 | 2 | 37.833 | 51.163 | .000 |
| Within Groups | 34.755 | 47 | .739 | | |
| Total | 110.420 | 49 | | | |

## Post Hoc Tests

### Multiple Comparisons

**Dependent Variable: IntelligentW1**

**LSD**

| (I) Education | (J) Education | Mean Difference (I–J) | Std. Error | Sig. | 95% Confidence Interval Lower Bound | 95% Confidence Interval Upper Bound |
|---|---|---|---|---|---|---|
| High School grad | college grad | −1.855* | .266 | .000 | −2.39 | −1.32 |
| | Master's grad | −3.400* | .360 | .000 | −4.12 | −2.68 |
| College grad | high school grad | 1.855* | .266 | .000 | 1.32 | 2.39 |
| | Master's grad | −1.545* | .355 | .000 | −2.26 | −.83 |
| Master's grad | high school grad | 3.400* | .360 | .000 | 2.68 | 4.12 |
| | college grad | 1.545* | .355 | .000 | .83 | 2.26 |

*The mean difference is significant at the .05 level.

## Means Plots

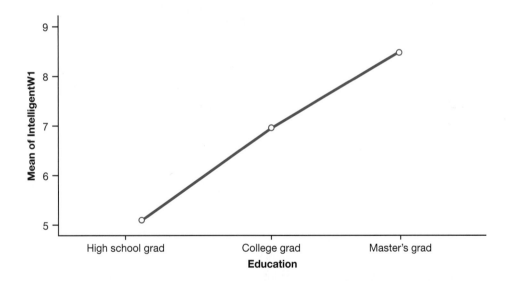

Just like in the independent-samples *t* test, in the first table called *Descriptives*, SPSS provides standard descriptive statistics for the dependent variable for each group separately. For this data, we can see that the 20 participants who saw Woman 1 with a high school degree rated her intelligence on average at 5.10, out of a possible 10, plus or minus the standard deviation of .91 (highlighted in the *Descriptives* table); the 22 participants who saw the same woman with a college degree rated her intelligence on average at 6.5, plus or minus the standard deviation of .79; and the 8 participants who saw Woman 1 with a master's degree rated her intelligence

*Interpretation* 4.2

at 8.50, plus or minus .93. So, we can see that the average intelligence rating was highest for the woman with the master's degree, followed by the woman with the college degree, then the woman with the high school degree. Furthermore, we can see that this difference was significant. In the *ANOVA* table, we can see that the *F* value, the degrees of freedom, and the *p* value (called *Sig.*) show there is a significant difference in the means because the *p* value is < .001, which is less than .05. This tells us that mean intelligence rating was significantly different among the three groups overall. We then use the Multiple Comparisons table to see where those specific differences are. Because all of the comparisons in this table are significant (all *p* values = .000), we can say that there are significant differences in mean intelligence rating among each of the education levels, with the master's degree rating being significantly higher than both the college and high school degree ratings, and a college degree rating being significantly higher than a high school degree rating.

**APA Style 4.2**

In order to report this one-way ANOVA using APA style, we will need the means and standard deviations for all three groups, as well as the *F* value, degrees of freedom, and *p* value (under *Sig.*). In addition, we will need to calculate a measure of effect size, called *eta squared* ($\eta^2$). This is a statistic that needs to be hand-calculated for the one-way ANOVA using the following formula:

$$\eta^2 = \frac{SSbetween}{SStotal}$$

You will need to find the SSbetween (*Sums of Squares Between Groups*) and the SStotal (*Sums of Squares Total*) from the *ANOVA* output, and divide those values. For this problem, the calculations for $\eta^2$ are:

$$\eta^2 = \frac{SSbetween}{SStotal} = \frac{76.67}{110.42} = .685$$

So, your APA-style Results paragraph should look like this:

A one-way analysis of variance was conducted to evaluate the relationship between education level and intelligence ratings. We hypothesized that there would be a significant difference in rating of intelligence (on a scale from 1 to 10) for the woman in the first photograph among the groups who saw her with a high school degree, college degree, and Master's degree. As predicted, education level significantly affected rating of intelligence $F(2, 47) = 51.16, p < .001$, $\eta^2 = .685$. Differences in education level explained 68.5% of the variance in intelligence rating. Follow-up tests were conducted to evaluate pairwise differences among the means and all were found to be significant (all *p*s < .001). The highest average intelligence rating was for the group who saw her with a master's degree ($M = 8.50, SD = .93$) compared to those who saw her with a college degree ($M = 6.95, SD = .79$) or a high school degree ($M = 5.10, SD = .91$).

# 4.3 Testing Within-Group Experimental Differences: Paired-Samples *T* Tests

When all participants receive all the levels of an independent variable, this is called a *within-groups experiment.* To test a within-groups design, in our example, researchers showed participants the picture of Woman 1 (who is dressed more casually) and then the picture of Woman 2 (who is dressed more professionally) to compare their ratings of intelligence for each of these women. Returning to our original example for this chapter in Section 4.1, researchers hypothesized that there would be within-group differences between the intelligence rating of Woman 1 and Woman 2. To test this hypothesis, we will use a paired-samples *t* test, where the independent variable is a categorical measure of photo shown (two levels: Woman 1 and Woman 2), and the dependent variable is the quantitative measure of each woman's intelligence, rated on a scale of 1 to 10. This is a within-groups test because all participants saw both pictures of the women. Here is how we would test to see if there is a significant difference in mean intelligence ratings for Woman 1 compared to Woman 2.

## THE DATA

In the third phase of the experiment discussed in Sections 4.1 and 4.2, researchers were interested in whether participants would rate Woman 1 (dressed more casually) differently from Woman 2 (dressed more professionally). They were instructed to rate each woman's intelligence on a scale of 1 (*not at all intelligent*) to 10 (*extremely intelligent*). This rating was the dependent variable. The researchers hypothesized that participants would rate Woman 2 as significantly more intelligent than Woman 1. Here is what the experiment looked like:

_____          _____

Please write your response on the line below each picture, rating the intelligence of each person in the photograph on a scale of 1 to 10 (where 1 is *not at all intelligent* and 10 is *extremely intelligent*). Note: Participants saw each picture separately.

When we entered the data into SPSS, we named the intelligence rating of Woman 1, *IntelligenceW1*, and the intelligence rating of Woman 2, *IntelligenceW2*.

Here's what the data look like in *Data View*:

| File | Edit | View | Data | Transform | Analyze | Direct Marketing | Graphs | Utilities |
|------|------|------|------|-----------|---------|------------------|--------|-----------|

| | Group | Education | HaveTattoo | IntelligentW1 | IntelligentW2 |
|----|-------|-----------|------------|---------------|---------------|
| 1 | 1 | 2 | 1 | 7 | 8 |
| 2 | 1 | 1 | 2 | 6 | 6 |
| 3 | 1 | 3 | 2 | 9 | 8 |
| 4 | 1 | 2 | 2 | 7 | 8 |
| 5 | 1 | 1 | 1 | 5 | 6 |
| 6 | 1 | 2 | 1 | 8 | 7 |
| 7 | 1 | 2 | 2 | 7 | 7 |
| 8 | 1 | 1 | 1 | 6 | 7 |
| 9 | 1 | 1 | 2 | 6 | 8 |
| 10 | 1 | 2 | 1 | 7 | 7 |
| 11 | 1 | 2 | 2 | 8 | 8 |
| 12 | 1 | 1 | 2 | 5 | 6 |
| 13 | 1 | 2 | 2 | 7 | 9 |
| 14 | 1 | 2 | 1 | 7 | 8 |
| 15 | 1 | 1 | 1 | 6 | 8 |
| 16 | 1 | 1 | 1 | 6 | 7 |
| 17 | 1 | 1 | 1 | 5 | 7 |
| 18 | 1 | 2 | 1 | 8 | 10 |
| 19 | 1 | 3 | 2 | 9 | 9 |
| 20 | 1 | 3 | 1 | 10 | 10 |
| 21 | 1 | 1 | 1 | 6 | 8 |

Data View | Variable View

Select from the Top Menu Bar:

ANALYZE → COMPARE MEANS → PAIRED-SAMPLE T TEST

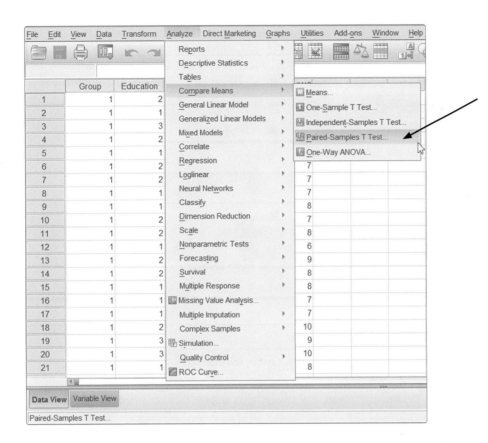

In the *Paired-Samples T Test* pop-up window, you would highlight the first variable and click the arrow pointing to *Pair 1 Variable1* cell, and highlight the second variable and click the arrow pointing to the *Pair 1 Variable2* cell. In my example, I clicked *IntelligenceW1* into *Variable1* and *IntelligenceW2* into *Variable2*. Then click 🆗.

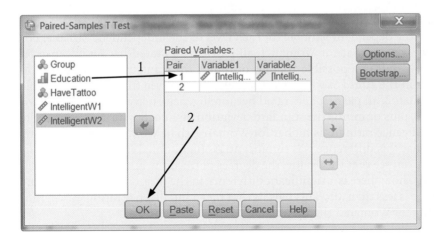

Testing Within-Group Experimental Differences: Paired-Samples *T* Tests

This is what the SPSS output looks like from the Paired-samples *t* test.

## *T* Test

### Paired Samples Statistics

| | | Mean | N | Std. Deviation | Std. Error Mean |
|---|---|---|---|---|---|
| Pair 1 | IntelligentW1 | 6.46 | 50 | 1.501 | .212 |
| | IntelligentW2 | 7.70 | 50 | 1.035 | .146 |

### Paired Samples Correlations

| | | N | Correlation | Sig. |
|---|---|---|---|---|
| Pair 1 | IntelligentW1 & IntelligentW2 | 50 | .590 | .000 |

### Paired Samples Test

| | | Paired Differences | | | | | | | |
|---|---|---|---|---|---|---|---|---|---|
| | | | | | 95% Confidence Interval of the Difference | | | | |
| | | Mean | Std. Deviation | Std. Error Mean | Lower | Upper | t | df | Sig. (2-tailed) |
| Pair 1 | IntelligentW1 – IntelligentW2 | −1.240 | 1.222 | .173 | −1.587 | −.893 | −7.178 | 49 | .000 |

In the first table, called *Paired Samples Statistics*, SPSS provides standard descriptive statistics for the dependent variable for each level of the independent variable. For this data, we can see that for Woman 1, all participants rated her intelligence on average at 6.46, out of a possible 10, plus or minus the standard deviation of 1.50 (highlighted in the *Paired Samples Statistics* table). We can see from that same table that for Woman 2, all participants rated her intelligence on average at 7.70, out of a possible 10, plus or minus the standard deviation of 1.04. So, we can see that the average intelligence rating was higher for Woman 2 than Woman 1. Furthermore, we can see that this difference was significant. As highlighted in the *Paired Samples Test* table, we can see that the *t* value, the degrees of freedom, and the *p* value [called *Sig. (2-tailed)*] show there is a significant difference in the means because the *p* value is .000, which is less than .05. This tells us that mean intelligence rating was significantly higher for Woman 2 than Woman 1.

In addition, SPSS also provides the correlation between participants' ratings of Woman 1 and Woman 2. In the second table, called *Paired Samples Correlations*, the Pearson correlation was .59, which is moderately strong, and significant, according to the *p* value (under *Sig.*) as highlighted in the table. This tells us that ratings for Woman 1 were significantly correlated with ratings for Woman 2, so those participants who rated Woman 1 as more intelligent were also likely to rate Woman 2 as more intelligent. One of the benefits of using a within-groups design is that it allows some control over individual differences. If we had done this experiment using a between-groups design and found that the group of participants who saw Woman 1 was in some way significantly different than the group of participants who saw Woman 2, then our between-groups experiment would have a fatal flaw. For instance, if the participants who saw Woman 1 were more likely to be employed in a corporate job than the participants who saw Woman 2, that could be a confound that already existed that would impact their ratings and the results of the experiment. However, when participants see both women, it is a true comparison of differences in their ratings without having to worry about differences in the participants themselves.

*APA Style*
**4.3**

In order to report the results of this test using APA style, we will need the means and standard deviations for both levels of the independent variable, as well as the *t* value, degrees of freedom, and *p* value [under *Sig.* (*2-tailed*)]. In addition, we will need to calculate the of effect size, called *d*. Again, this is a statistic that needs to be hand-calculated using the following formula (which is different from the independent-samples *d* formula):

$$d = \frac{Mean\,difference}{Standard\,deviation}$$

For this problem, the calculations for *d* are:

$$d = \frac{-1.24}{1.22} = -1.02$$

So, your APA-style Results paragraph should look like this:

> We hypothesized that there would be a significant difference in the rating of intelligence (on a scale from 1 to 10) for the woman in the first photograph compared to the rating of intelligence for the woman in the second photograph, as rated by the same participants. As predicted, rating of intelligence was significantly higher on average for Woman 2 ($M = 7.70$, $SD = 1.04$) compared to Woman 1 ($M = 6.46$, $SD = 1.50$), $t(49) = -7.18$, $p < .001$, $d = -1.02$.

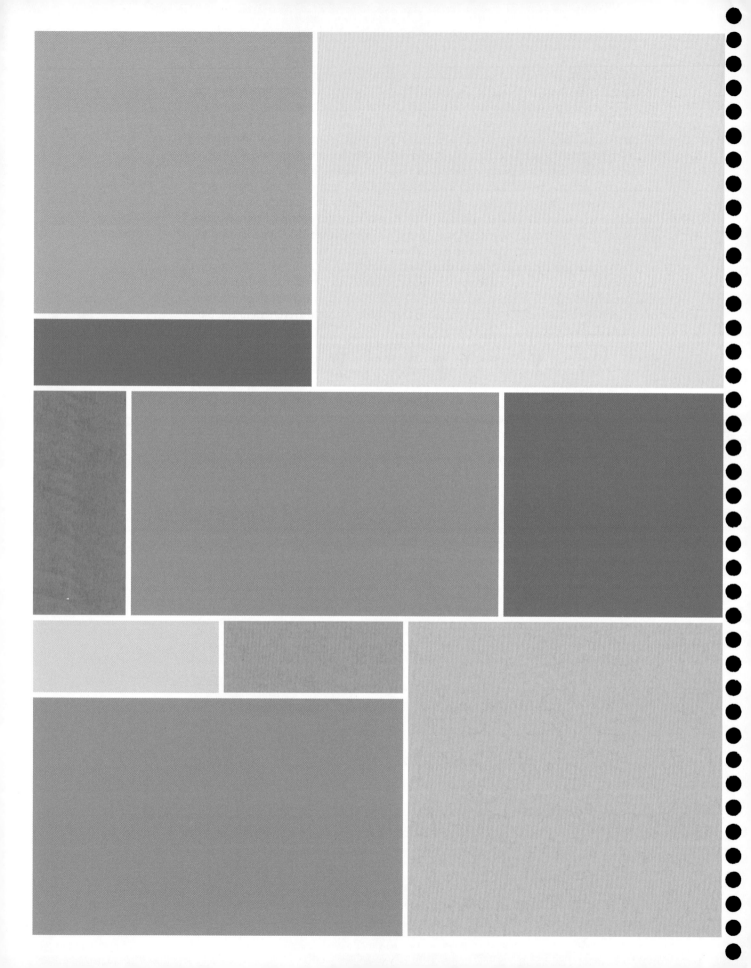

# 5

## Taking It Up a Notch

### Multivariate Experiments with Analysis of Variance

*When the complexity of comparing means goes beyond two sample means or just one independent variable (as in Chapter 4), you should use more complex forms of ANOVA. This chapter will cover the basics of ANOVA with multiple independent variables, including testing for sample mean differences considering the combined effect of two independent variables (factorial), looking at main effects and interactions, and using more complex designs involving paired data (repeated measures).*

The data we will use for this first part of this chapter are the same data used in Chapter 4, Section 1, where the researchers were interested in whether tattoos impacted perceptions of intelligence, specifically for the picture of Woman 1. In this experiment, participants were randomly assigned to see photographs of women (one at a time): the first group seeing Woman 1 without a tattoo (see below on the left), and the second group seeing Woman 1 with a tattoo (see below on the right). The independent variable is tattoo condition because the researchers manipulated it. There are two levels of the tattoo condition: no tattoo versus a tattoo on her arm. Participants were instructed to rate the woman's intelligence on a scale of 1 (*not at all intelligent*) to 10 (*extremely intelligent*). This rating was the dependent variable. Participants also indicated whether or not they had a tattoo themselves. Whether or not participants had a tattoo is going to serve as our second independent variable in this chapter. The researchers hypothesized that Woman 1 with a tattoo would be rated higher in intelligence by participants with a tattoo than by participants without a tattoo. This rating would not be as high as the rating for Woman 1 without a tattoo regardless of whether the participant had a tattoo. Here is what the experiment looked like:

**Woman 1 without tattoo**

**Woman 1 with tattoo**

Please write your response on the line below the picture, rating the intelligence of the person in the photograph on a scale of 1 to 10 (where 1 is *not at all intelligent* and 10 is *extremely intelligent*).

Do you have one or more tattoos on your body?　　　　YES　　　　NO

When entering this data into IBM SPSS Statistics software ("SPSS"), the first variable entered was the photograph group to which participants belonged. I named this variable *Group*, with 1 being the woman with *no tattoo* group and 2 being the woman with a *tattoo* group. Second, we entered the answer to the question about whether the participant had a tattoo, which I named *HaveTattoo*. *HaveTatto* was coded as a 1 for *don't have a tattoo* and a 2 for *have a tattoo*. Finally, we entered in their intelligence rating for Woman 1, named *IntelligenceW1*. This is what the data look like in *Data View* in SPSS.

| File | Edit | View | Data | Transform | Analyze | Direct Marketing | Graphs | Utilities |
|---|---|---|---|---|---|---|---|---|

|  | Group | HaveTattoo | IntelligentW 1 | IntelligentW 2 | var | var |
|---|---|---|---|---|---|---|
| 1 | 1 | 1 | 7 | 8 | | |
| 2 | 1 | 2 | 6 | 6 | | |
| 3 | 1 | 2 | 9 | 8 | | |
| 4 | 1 | 2 | 7 | 8 | | |
| 5 | 1 | 1 | 5 | 6 | | |
| 6 | 1 | 1 | 8 | 7 | | |
| 7 | 1 | 2 | 7 | 7 | | |
| 8 | 1 | 1 | 6 | 7 | | |
| 9 | 1 | 2 | 6 | 8 | | |
| 10 | 1 | 1 | 7 | 7 | | |
| 11 | 1 | 2 | 8 | 8 | | |
| 12 | 1 | 2 | 5 | 6 | | |
| 13 | 1 | 2 | 7 | 9 | | |
| 14 | 1 | 1 | 7 | 8 | | |
| 15 | 1 | 1 | 6 | 8 | | |
| 16 | 1 | 1 | 6 | 7 | | |
| 17 | 1 | 1 | 5 | 7 | | |
| 18 | 1 | 1 | 8 | 10 | | |
| 19 | 1 | 2 | 9 | 9 | | |
| 20 | 1 | 1 | 10 | 10 | | |
| 21 | 1 | 1 | 6 | 8 | | |

Data View | Variable View

# Before We Get Started: Between-Groups versus Within-Groups Designs

As in Chapter 4, there are two ways to test multivariate experiments: between-groups or within-groups. In between-groups experiments, researchers randomly assign participants to independent groups and then expose one group to one level of the independent variable and the other groups to the other level of the independent variable. In within-groups experiments, participants are exposed to all the levels of the independent variable. We will cover both between-groups designs and within-groups designs in this chapter.

## 5.1 Testing Complex Between-Group Experimental Differences: Factorial ANOVA

When participants are randomly assigned to groups where each receive different levels of an independent variable, this is called a between-groups experiment. In our particular example for this chapter, participants are randomly assigned to see a photograph of the same person, specifically Woman 1 with or without a tattoo. In Chapter 4, we already tested to see if there was a significant difference between these two groups on their ratings of intelligence for Woman 1 with the tattoo versus Woman 1 without the tattoo using an independent-samples *t* test. However, if we would like to add to this test to see if the participants having a tattoo themselves impacted the intelligence ratings, in addition to the photograph tattoo condition, then a more complex analysis would be needed, called *factorial ANOVA*. We need factorial ANOVA because we now have more than one independent variable or factor: we have whether or not Woman 1 is shown with a tattoo (the experimentally manipulated independent variable, named *Group*), and whether the participant has a tattoo themselves (the quasi-experimental independent variable, named *HaveTattoo*). The variable *HaveTattoo* is a quasi-experimental factor because it was not manipulated. Rather, *HaveTattoo* occurred naturally. Sometimes when we talk about variables like this, we say participants self-selected, so it is not a full-fledged experimental factor. A factorial ANOVA allows us to test the impact of both of these variables simultaneously.

In addition, we can also see if there is a moderating relationship by testing the interaction between these two factors. An interaction exists if there is a moderating relationship: one independent variable changes the relationship between another independent variable and the dependent variable. In our example, we can test to see if rating of intelligence for Woman 1 (dependent variable) with and without the tattoo (independent variable) is different for the participants with a tattoo themselves (moderating independent variable). In other words, do people with a tattoo rate others (with or without a tattoo) differently than people without a tattoo? The researchers hypothesized that for participants with a tattoo, Woman 1 with a tattoo would be rated higher in intelliegence than for participants without a tattoo. This rating would not be as high as the rating for Woman 1 without a tattoo regardless of whether the participant had a tattoo.

Therefore, we are testing two types of hypotheses with factorial ANOVA. First, we are testing what we call "main effects"—namely, the effects of each of the independent variables overall on the dependent variable. There are two potential main effects in our study: the impact of whether Woman 1 has a tattoo on intelligence ratings, and the impact of the participant having a tattoo on intelligence ratings. Second, we are testing an "interaction effect"—that is, whether the impact of one factor depends on the level of the other factor. Specifically, we are testing intelligence ratings for Woman 1 with and without a tattoo interacting with participants having or not having a tattoo. Here are the commands to run a factorial ANOVA, with *Group* and *HaveTattoo* as independent variables (factors) and *IntelligenceW1* as the dependent variable.

Select from the Top Menu Bar:

SPSS Commands
5.1

ANALYZE → GENERAL LINEAR MODEL → UNIVARIATE

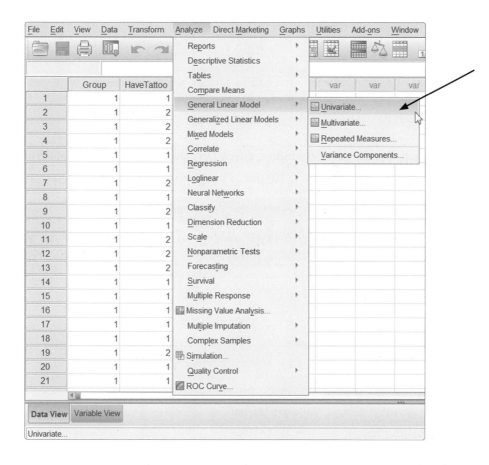

In the *Univariate* pop-up window, highlight *IntelligentW1* and click the arrow point-ing to the *Dependent Variable* box, and highlight both *Group* and *HaveTattoo* and click the arrow pointing to the *Fixed Factor(s)* box, then select the **Options...** button.

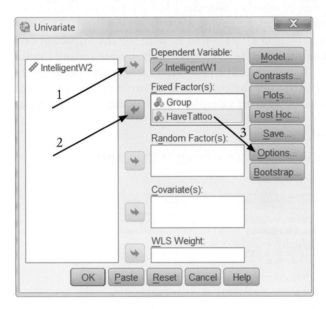

In the *Univariate: Options* pop-up window, check *Descriptive Statistics* and *Estimates of Effect Size*, then click **Continue**.

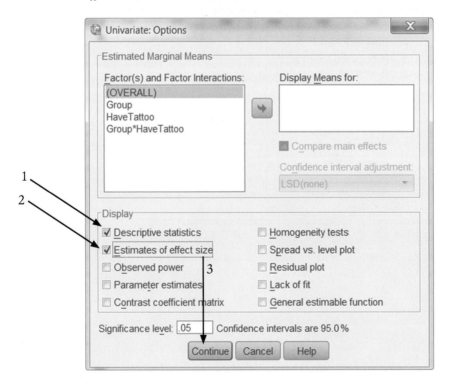

Then, in the *Univariate* pop-up window, again, select the [Plots...] button.

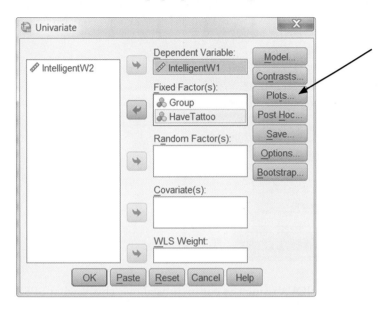

In the *Univariate: Profile Plots* pop-up window, highlight *Group* and click the arrow pointing to the *Horizontal Axis* box, and highlight *HaveTattoo* and click the arrow pointing to the *Separate Lines* box, and click [Add], then click [Continue], then click [OK]. The variable you put as the *Horizontal Axis* and *Separate Lines* is a personal preference. I put *Group* on the *Horizontal Axis* so that the two conditions of tattoo for Woman 1 would be in separate groups on the x-axis, and then I put *HaveTattoo* in the *Separate Lines* box so that *HaveTattoo* would be represented by two lines in the graph: one line for participants who had a tattoo, and one line for participants who did not have a tattoo.

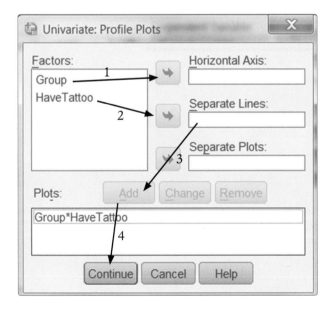

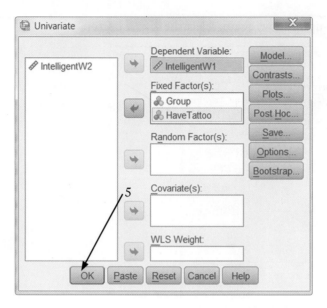

When you run the factorial ANOVA using the commands above, this is what SPSS provides.

## Univariate Analysis of Variance

### Between-Subjects Factors

|  |  | Value Label | N |
|---|---|---|---|
| Group | 1 | No Tattoos | 25 |
|  | 2 | Tattoos | 25 |
| HaveTattoo | 1 | Don't have a tattoo | 26 |
|  | 2 | Do have a tattoo | 24 |

## Descriptive Statistics

**Dependent Variable: IntelligentW1**

| Group | HaveTattoo | Mean | Std. Deviation | N |
|---|---|---|---|---|
| No Tattoos | Don't have a tattoo | 6.69 | 1.377 | 13 |
| | Do have a tattoo | 7.17 | 1.193 | 12 |
| | Total | 6.92 | 1.288 | 25 |
| Tattoos | Don't have a tattoo | 4.77 | .927 | 13 |
| | Do have a tattoo | 7.33 | .888 | 12 |
| | Total | 6.00 | 1.581 | 25 |
| Total | Don't have a tattoo | 5.73 | 1.511 | 26 |
| | Do have a tattoo | 7.25 | 1.032 | 24 |
| | Total | 6.46 | 1.501 | 50 |

## Tests of Between-Subjects Effects

**Dependent Variable: IntelligentW1**

| Source | Type III Sum of Squares | df | Mean Square | F | Sig. | Partial Eta Squared |
|---|---|---|---|---|---|---|
| Corrected Model | 53.010[a] | 3 | 17.670 | 14.158 | .000 | .480 |
| Intercept | 2102.885 | 1 | 2102.885 | 1684.937 | .000 | .973 |
| Group | 9.625 | 1 | 9.625 | 7.712 | .008 | .144 |
| HaveTattoo | 28.805 | 1 | 28.805 | 23.080 | .000 | .334 |
| Group * HaveTattoo | 13.625 | 1 | 13.625 | 10.917 | .002 | .192 |
| Error | 57.410 | 46 | 1.248 | | | |
| Total | 2197.000 | 50 | | | | |
| Corrected Total | 110.420 | 49 | | | | |

a. R Squared = .480 (Adjusted R Squared = .446)

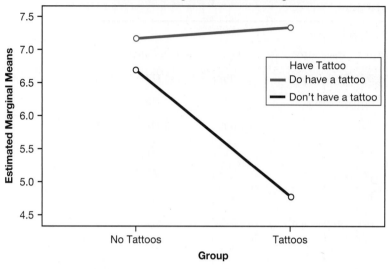

**Estimated Marginal Means of IntelligentW1**

*Interpretation*
**5.1**

The first table shows us how many participants are in each condition. The second table reports descriptive statistics, including the means and standard deviations for both the main effects (*Group* and *HaveTattoo*, individually) and the interaction effect (*Group\*HaveTattoo*). The third table tests for significance (listed under under *Sig.*) for both main effects (*Group* and *HaveTattoo*, individually) and the interaction effect (*Group\*HaveTattoo*). Both main effects and the interaction are significant (all *p*s < .05). For the main effect of photograph tattoo condition, participants (regardless of whether they had a tattoo themselves) who saw Woman 1 with no tattoo rated her at 6.92 (*SD* = 1.29). This was significantly higher than participants who saw Woman 1 with a tattoo, who rated her at 6.00 (*SD* = 1.58), *p* = .008. For the main effect of participant tattoo condition, participants with no tattoo rated Woman 1 (regardless of whether she was pictured with a tattoo or not) at 5.73 (*SD* = 1.51). This was significantly lower than participants with a tattoo, who rated her at 7.25 (*SD* = 1.03), *p* < .000. In addition, the interaction was significant at *p* = .002.

The interaction is easier to understand if you look at the graph showing that for the sample who saw Woman 1 without a tattoo, there were no significant differences in her intelligence rating for participants who had a tattoo or not. This shows that participants who saw the picture of Woman 1 without a tattoo rated her about the same, regardless of whether they themselves had a tattoo (*M* = 7.17, *SD* = 1.19) or didn't have a tattoo (*M* = 6.69, *SD* = 1.38). In contrast, when Woman 1 was shown with a tattoo, there was a significant difference in intelligence rating, with participants who have a tattoo rating her intelligence significantly higher with a mean of 7.33 (*SD* = .89), than participants without a tattoo with a mean of 4.77 (*SD* = .93). This shows that participants with a tattoo rated Woman 1 pictured with a tattoo more positively than did participants who don't have a tattoo, showing that perhaps tattooed participants identified with the person pictured with a tattoo more than did the participants without a tattoo.

In order to report these findings in words in APA style for a Results section, you will need several pieces of information. You will need the means and standard deviations, *F* value, degrees of freedom, *p* value (*Sig.*), and partial eta squared value for both main effects and the interaction. Partial eta squared is a measure of effect size that SPSS provides, so we don't need to calculate it like we did in other chapters. Here is what your results would look like in APA style:

> To investigate the effect of tattoos on perceived intelligence, we ran a two-way ANOVA. We investigated the effect of tattoos both on a model viewed in a photograph and on the participants themselves. The photograph tattoo condition and participant tattoo condition were the factors and intelligence rating was the dependent variable in the model. There was a significant main effect of photograph tattoo condition with participants who saw Woman 1 with no tattoo ($M = 6.92$, $SD = 1.29$) rating her intelligence significantly higher than participants who saw Woman 1 with a tattoo ($M = 6.00$, $SD = 1.58$), $F(1, 46) = 7.71$, $p = .008$, $\eta_p^2 = .144$. For the main effect of participant tattoo condition, participants with no tattoo rated Woman 1 ($M = 5.73$, $SD = 1.51$) significantly lower on intelligence than participants with a tattoo ($M = 7.25$, $SD = 1.03$), $F(1, 46) = 23.08$, $p < .001$, $\eta_p^2 = .334$. In addition, the photograph tattoo condition × participant tattoo condition interaction was significant, $F(1, 46) = 10.92$, $p = .002$, $\eta_p^2 = .192$. Intelligence ratings for Woman 1 without a tattoo were similar for participants who had a tattoo themselves ($M = 7.17$, $SD = 1.19$) and those who did not ($M = 6.69$, $SD = 1.38$). However, when Woman 1 was shown with a tattoo there was a difference in intelligence rating with participants who have a tattoo rating her intelligence higher ($M = 7.33$, $SD = .89$) than participants without a tattoo ($M = 4.77$, $SD = .93$).

## 5.1a  Graphing an Interaction

When you run a factorial ANOVA and find a significant interaction, you may choose to graph it with a bar chart of means, including the confidence intervals to show the significant differences graphically. Showing the confidence intervals helps to determine if the differences between the means are statistically significant. When the confidence intervals do not overlap in the graph, then those means would be considered statistically significant. To make a bar chart of means in SPSS, follow the instructions below.

Select from the Top Menu Bar:

GRAPHS → CHART BUILDER

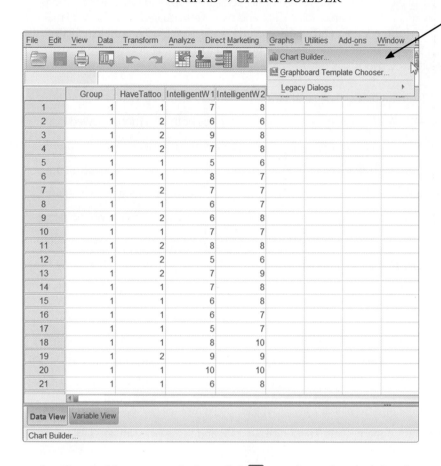

In the *Chart Builder* pop-up window, click **OK** as we have already defined our variables.

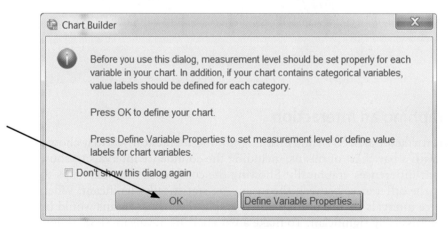

In the next *Chart Builder* pop-up window, under *Gallery*, choose *Bar*, then choose *Clustered Bar* (the second from the top left choice in the Gallery).

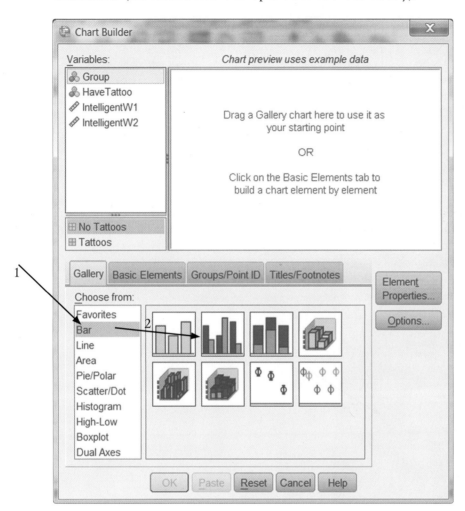

Next, while still in the *Chart Builder* pop-up window, on the top under *Variables* and the *Chart Preview*, drag *IntelligenceW1* from the *Variables* box into the y-axis on the *Chart Preview* graph, *Group* from the *Variables* box into the x-axis on the *Chart Preview* graph, and *HaveTattoo* from the *Variables* box into the *Cluster on X* box. The dependent variable (*IntelligenceW1*) belongs on the y-axis, and then you can choose the independent variable you would like on the x-axis (*Group* for my choice) and the independent variable you would like represented by the different colored bars (*HaveTattoo* for my choice).

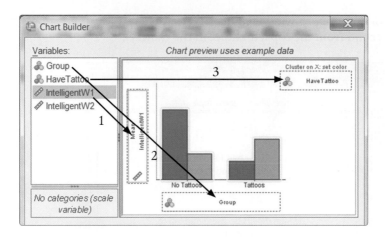

Finally, click on the *Element Properties* pop-up window that shows to the right, check *Display error bars*, then click Apply down at the bottom right, then click OK.

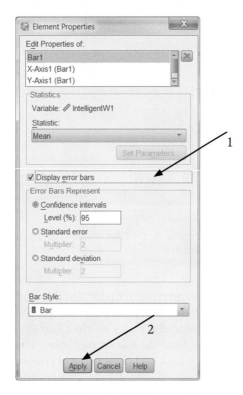

Like this:

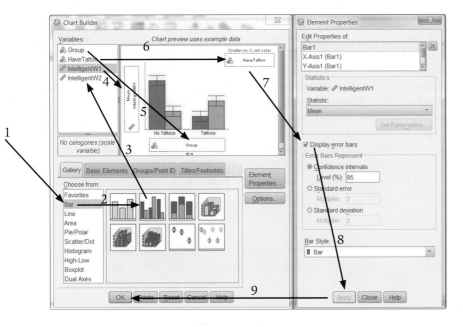

When you follow these instructions, SPSS will make a bar graph like the one shown below.

*SPSS Output*
**5.1a**

Confidence Intervals overlap (not significant)

Confidence Intervals don't overlap (significant)

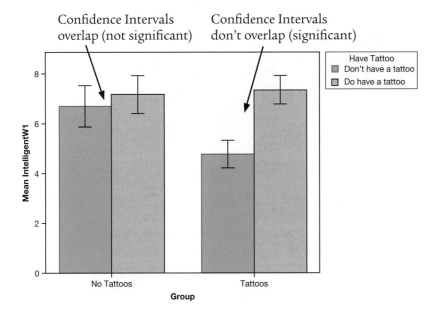

This bar graph shows the mean intelligence rating for each level of both *Group* and *HaveTattoo*. In the first two bars (no tattoos on the photographs) the confidence interval bars overlap, and there is not a significant difference in mean intelligence rating between participants with or without a tattoo when they view Woman 1 without a tattoo. However, because the confidence interval bars do not overlap in the Tattoos condition (two bars on the right of the graph), this shows that there is a significant difference in mean intelligence rating for participants with or without a tattoo when they view Woman 1 with a tattoo. Participants who don't have a tattoo themselves rated the intelligence of Woman 1 significantly lower when she is shown with a tattoo than participants who have a tattoo themselves. This shows that having a tattoo increases your perception of a tattooed person's intelligence as compared to a person who doesn't have a tattoo. Another way to say this is that not having a tattoo makes you more likely to discount someone's intelligence if you see that she does have a tattoo.

In addition to the text reporting the findings from this factorial ANOVA as in the previous section (5.1), here is a way to present the SPSS bar graph in APA style.

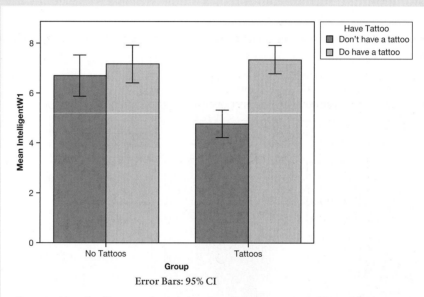

*Figure 5.1* Mean intelligence rating as a function of picture tattoo condition and participant tattoo condition.

## 5.2 Testing Complex Within-Group Experimental Differences: Repeated Measures ANOVA

When participants receive all the different levels of an independent variable, this is called a *within-groups experiment*. Building on our example for this chapter, all participants viewed all four photographs: two women and two men (we have previously just looked at Woman 1). In Chapter 4, we tested to see if there was a significant difference in mean intelligence ratings between Woman 1 and Woman 2 using a paired-samples *t* test. However, the paired-samples *t* test is limited and only allows us to compare two means. If we wanted to see if there was a significant difference between all four mean intelligence ratings, we would have to use the more powerful Repeated Measures ANOVA.

### THE DATA

The data we will use for this part of the chapter builds on the data used before, where the researchers were interested in intelligence ratings of people in photographs. In this within-groups experiment, participants rated four pictures: two pictures of women (the same as the example in Chapter 4) and two pictures of men. They were instructed to rate each person's intelligence on a scale of 1 (*not at all intelligent*) to 10 (*extremely intelligent*). Participants saw each picture separately. Here is what the experiment looked like:

Please write your response below each picture, rating the intelligence of each person in the photograph on a scale of 1 to 10 (where 1 is *not at all intelligent* and 10 is *extremely intelligent*). Note: Each photograph was viewed separately.

When entering this data into SPSS, we entered some other relevant variables from the experiment that were used elsewhere, like *Group* and *HaveTattoo*, but most importantly for this analysis, we entered the four intelligence ratings: Woman 1 (called *IntelligenceW1*), Woman 2 (called *IntelligenceW2*), Man 1 (called *IntelligenceM1*), and Man 2 (called *IntelligenceM2*).

This is what the data look like in *Data View* in SPSS.

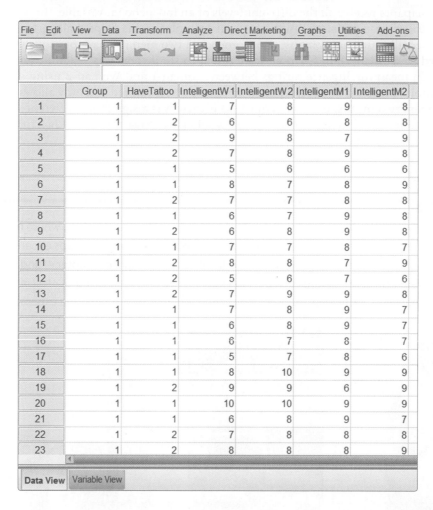

Because all participants rated all four photographs, this is a within-groups design. The researchers hypothesized that Man 1, who is dressed more professionally, would be rated highest on intelligence, while the more casually dressed Woman 1 would be rated lowest on intelligence. We ran a repeated measures ANOVA to test for differences in intelligence ratings of the people in the four photographs using the following SPSS commands:

Select from the Top Menu Bar:

ANALYZE → GENERAL LINEAR MODEL → REPEATED MEASURES

In the *Repeated Measures Define Factor* pop-up window, type in the number of repeated measurements you have in the *Number of Levels* box, then click Add, then click Define.

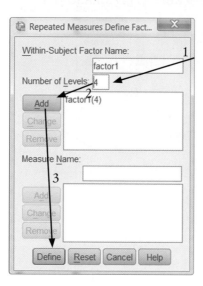

In the *Repeated Measures* pop-up window, highlight *IntelligenceW1*, *IntelligenceW2*, *IntelligenceM1*, and *IntelligenceM2*, and click the arrow pointing to the *Within-Subject Variables (factor1)* box, then click Options....

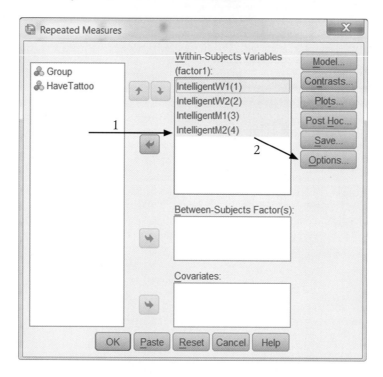

In the *Repeated Measures: Options* pop-up window, highlight *factor1* and click the arrow pointing to the *Display means for:* window, and check the box *Compare main effects*. Then, check *Descriptive statistics* and *Estimates of effect size* and then click Continue , then click OK .

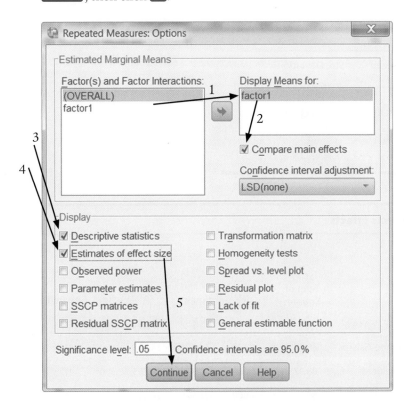

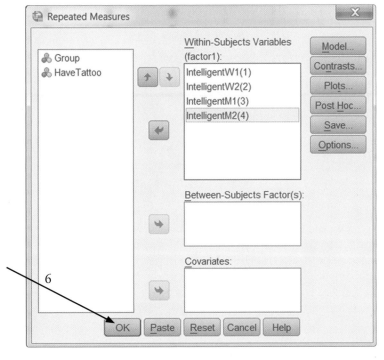

When you run this repeated measures ANOVA using these commands, SPSS gives you a lot of output. You only really need these tables below.

## General Linear Model

### Descriptive Statistics

|  | Mean | Std. Deviation | N |
|---|---|---|---|
| IntelligentW1 | 6.46 | 1.501 | 50 |
| IntelligentW2 | 7.70 | 1.035 | 50 |
| IntelligentM1 | 8.28 | .757 | 50 |
| IntelligentM2 | 7.22 | 1.447 | 50 |

### Tests of Within-Subjects Effects

**Measure: MEASURE_1**

| Source |  | Type III Sum of Squares | df | Mean Square | F | Sig. | Partial Eta Squared |
|---|---|---|---|---|---|---|---|
| actor1 | Sphericity Assumed | 88.975 | 3 | 29.658 | 34.255 | .000 | .411 |
|  | Greenhouse-Geisser | 88.975 | 1.639 | 54.294 | 34.255 | .000 | .411 |
|  | Huynh-Feldt | 88.975 | 1.688 | 52.716 | 34.255 | .000 | .411 |
|  | Lower-bound | 88.975 | 1.000 | 88.975 | 34.255 | .000 | .411 |
| Error(factor1) | Sphericity Assumed | 127.275 | 147 | .866 |  |  |  |
|  | Greenhouse-Geisser | 127.275 | 80.299 | 1.585 |  |  |  |
|  | Huynh-Feldt | 127.275 | 82.703 | 1.539 |  |  |  |
|  | Lower-bound | 127.275 | 49.000 | 2.597 |  |  |  |

## Pairwise Comparisons

**Measure: MEASURE_1**

| (I) factor1 | (J) factor1 | Mean Difference (I-J) | Std. Error | Sig.[b] | 95% Confidence Interval for Difference[b] | |
|---|---|---|---|---|---|---|
| | | | | | Lower Bound | Upper Bound |
| 1 | 2 | −1.240* | .173 | .000 | −1.587 | −.893 |
| | 3 | −1.820* | .245 | .000 | −2.313 | −1.327 |
| | 4 | −.760* | .101 | .000 | −.963 | −.557 |
| 2 | 1 | 1.240* | .173 | .000 | .893 | 1.587 |
| | 3 | −.580* | .143 | .000 | −.868 | −.292 |
| | 4 | .480* | .181 | .011 | .116 | .844 |
| 3 | 1 | 1.820* | .245 | .000 | 1.327 | 2.313 |
| | 2 | .580* | .143 | .000 | .292 | .868 |
| | 4 | 1.060* | .233 | .000 | .592 | 1.528 |
| 4 | 1 | .760* | .101 | .000 | .557 | .963 |
| | 2 | −.480* | .181 | .011 | −.844 | −.116 |
| | 3 | −1.060* | .233 | .000 | −1.528 | −.592 |

Based on estimated marginal means

*The mean difference is significant at the .05 level.

b. Adjustment for multiple comparisons: Least Significant Difference (equivalent to no adjustments).

## Multivariate Tests[a]

| Effect | | Value | F | Hypothesis df | Error df | Sig. | Partial Eta Squared |
|---|---|---|---|---|---|---|---|
| factor1 | Pillai's Trace | .648 | 28.894[b] | 3.000 | 47.000 | .000 | .648 |
| | Wilks' Lambda | .352 | 28.894[b] | 3.000 | 47.000 | .000 | .648 |
| | Hotelling's Trace | 1.844 | 28.894[b] | 3.000 | 47.000 | .000 | .648 |
| | Roy's Largest Root | 1.844 | 28.894[b] | 3.000 | 47.000 | .000 | .648 |

a. Design: Intercept Within Subjects Design: factor1

b. Exact statistic

Pairwise Comparisons

The table called *Descriptive Statistics* shows the means and standard deviations of intelligence ratings for all four pictures. The second table called *Tests of Within-Subjects Effects* shows that the intelligence ratings among the four photographs were significantly different, because the *F* statistic has a *p* value that is less than .05 ($p < .001$).

The fourth table called *Multivariate Tests* also shows us that there is a significant difference in mean ratings of intelligence between the four photographed people, because the *Wilks's lambda* test has a *p* value that is less than .05 ($p < .001$). As you can see, the output provides several ways to test the hypothesis that there are significant differences in the intelligence ratings among the four photographs, and all show significant differences.

Finding an overall significance difference among the four photographs would lead us to want to test for significant differences between pairs of mean intelligence ratings. The third table, called *Pairwise Comparisons*, shows us the differences between ratings for each pair of pictures (e.g., between Woman 1 and Woman 2, between Woman 1 and Man 1). All of these pairwise comparison have a *p* value less than .05, showing that these pairwise differences are all significant (all *ps* < .05). This means that there are significant differences between each photograph and all the others for intelligence ratings, with Man 1 being rated the highest ($M = 8.28$, $SD = .76$), followed by Woman 2 ($M = 7.70$, $SD = 1.04$), Man 2 ($M = 7.22$, $SD = 1.45$), and finally, Woman 1 ($M = 6.46$, $SD = 1.50$). This coincides with the researcher's hypothesis that the more professionally dressed Man 1 would be rated highest on intelligence, and the more casually dressed Woman 1 would be rated lowest on intelligence.

*APA Style*
**5.2**

In order to write this Repeated Measures result in APA style, you will need several pieces of information. From the *Multivariate Tests* table, you will need the Wilks's lambda value; from the *Within-Subjects Effects* table, you will need the *F* value, degrees of freedom, *p* value, and eta squared value; and from the *Pairwise Comparisons* table, you will need the *p* values. This is how this finding would look in APA style:

A repeated measures ANOVA assessed differences in mean intelligence ratings among four photographed people. The means and standard deviations for the intelligence ratings are presented in Table 1. The results for the ANOVA indicate a significant difference in the mean ratings of the four photographs, Wilks's $\lambda = .35$, $F(3) = 34.26$, $p < .001$, $\eta^2 = .41$. All pairwise comparisons between means are significant (all *ps* < .05). As hypothesized, Man 1 was rated as the most intelligent and Woman 1 was rated as the least intelligent.

Table 1

*Means and Standard Deviations for Intelligence Ratings*

| Photograph | M | SD |
|---|---|---|
| Woman 1 | 6.46 | 1.50 |
| Woman 2 | 7.70 | 1.04 |
| Man 1 | 8.28 | .76 |
| Man 2 | 7.22 | 1.45 |

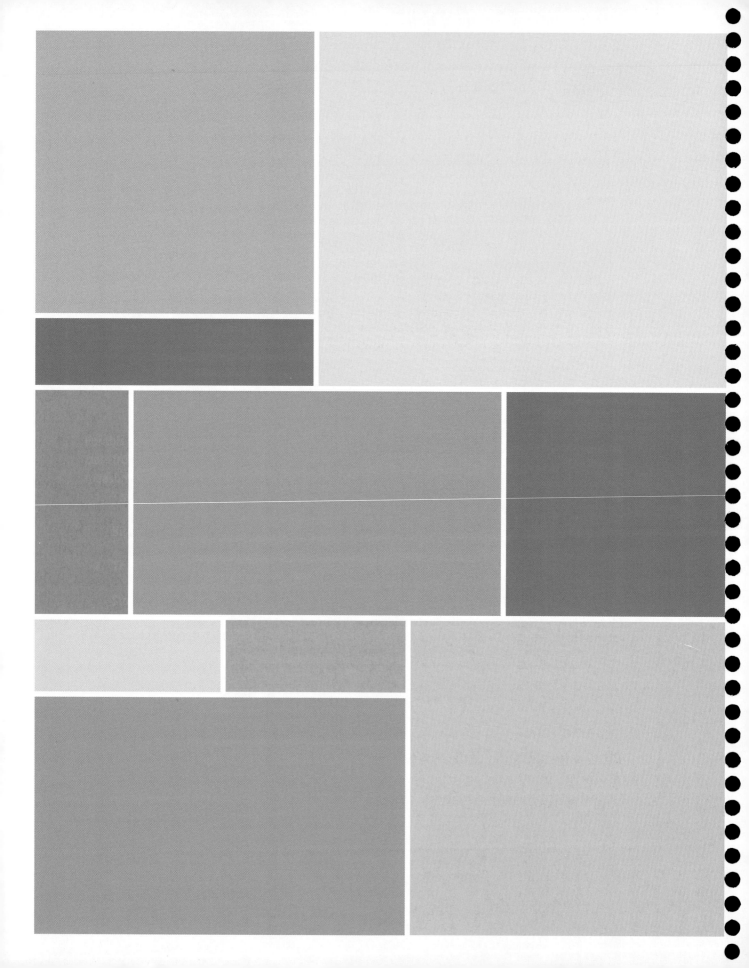

# 6

# Predicting Outcomes Using Multiple Regression

*Regression analyses provide a glimpse into how science begins to explain behavior by demonstrating how different variables can be used to predict outcomes. Multiple Regression allows you to statistically control for third variables when making association claims. In this chapter, you will learn multiple regression analyses, including testing for mediation and moderation.*

## THE DATA

In this chapter, we will use four variables collected from the 45 students in my research methods class. We used some of these questions in Chapter 3. We were interested in exploring what variables predicted GPA. We looked at motivation, IQ, and hours spent studying to see if they predicted the GPA of the students in my class. A survey asked them the following questions:

1. **On a scale of 1 to 100, where 1 is *not at all* and 100 is *extremely*, how motivated are you to achieve?**

   _____

2. **What is your approximate IQ score?**

   _____

3. **What is your cumulative GPA to the nearest tenth (example: round 3.094 to 3.1)?** _____._____

4. **In an average week, how many hours do you spend altogether doing the following: studying, reading school related materials, and doing homework?**

   _____ **hours**

Here's what these data look like in Data View:

| File | Edit | View | Data | Transform | Analyze | Direct Marketing |
|------|------|------|------|-----------|---------|------------------|

16 :

| | motscore | gpa | IQ | hrsstudy |
|----|----------|-----|-----|----------|
| 1 | 99 | 4.0 | 105 | 8 |
| 2 | 94 | 3.9 | 136 | 5 |
| 3 | 98 | 3.9 | 101 | 8 |
| 4 | 93 | 3.7 | 110 | 15 |
| 5 | 99 | 3.7 | 108 | 4 |
| 6 | 90 | 3.6 | 120 | 7 |
| 7 | 92 | 3.6 | 104 | 14 |
| 8 | 87 | 3.4 | 120 | 19 |
| 9 | 87 | 3.3 | 92 | 10 |
| 10 | 90 | 3.2 | 107 | 15 |
| 11 | 85 | 3.1 | 103 | 12 |
| 12 | 88 | 3.1 | 93 | 9 |
| 13 | 90 | 3.1 | 95 | 8 |
| 14 | 86 | 3.0 | 89 | 15 |
| 15 | 80 | 2.9 | 100 | 4 |
| 16 | 83 | 2.7 | 94 | 8 |
| 17 | 79 | 2.6 | 104 | 18 |
| 18 | 70 | 2.4 | 102 | 7 |
| 19 | 73 | 2.3 | 87 | 12 |
| 20 | 71 | 2.2 | 95 | 11 |
| 21 | 66 | 2.1 | 102 | 6 |
| 22 | 69 | 1.8 | 90 | 16 |
| 23 | 64 | 1.7 | 100 | 5 |

Data View | Variable View

# Before We Get Started: Types of Variables and Association Claims

In Chapters 4 and 5, we talked about ways to test causal claims. However, there are also some more complex ways to test association claims with multiple variables. In this chapter, we will use regression as a way to test more complex association claims. As we talked about previously in Chapter 3 with the correlation, regression is appropriate if you are testing associations with quantitative, numeric data. Also, the relationship that you are testing must be linear, not curvilinear. This means that as the first variable increases, the second variable must increase or decrease, but it must not increase first then decrease or change direction midway. Finally, regression can only test association claims (claiming that a relationship exists between the variables), but it cannot test that one variable causes the other. Causal claims need methods that manipulate a variable, and regression, although closer to ruling out other potential variables, is not an appropriate statistic to test causal claims.

## 6.1 Testing for Association among Multiple Variables: Multivariate Linear Regression

Correlation is a great way to measure the linear association between two variables (see Chapter 3). Regression helps us see the predictive effect of multiple independent variables (also called *predictors*) on a dependent variable (also called a *criterion*). In this way, regression helps us move one step closer to meeting the criteria needed to establish causation. Although regression is still testing association, it can help us to rule out a third-variable explanation by controlling for other variables in the model. In our example, we can test to see how motivation is associated with GPA, while controlling for IQ at the same time. Of course, it would be great if we could run an experiment to meet all three criteria for making a causal claim, but many times this isn't possible. For instance, if we wanted to do an experiment on whether having a higher IQ causes a higher GPA, that just wouldn't be possible. There are some variables, such as IQ, that are individual traits that we can't manipulate. In these situations, regression is an important analytic tool to understand IQ's relationship, along with motivation to GPA. Another way to think about regression is testing the relative influence of different variables on a dependent variable when more than one predictor might be significant.

We call it *multiple* linear regression because we have multiple predictors; we call it multiple *linear* regression because it is measuring a straight line or increase-increase, increase-decrease type relationship. We measure the association of these multiple predictor variables with the dependent variable by measuring the proportion of the total variance (or variability) in the dependent variable that is accounted for by each predictor, while controlling for the effects of each of the other predictors. Here's how to run a multiple regression with *GPA* (*gpa*) as the dependent variable, and motivational score (*motscore*), IQ (*iq*), and hours studied (*hrsstudy*) as the predictors.

Select from the Top Menu Bar:

*SPSS Commands*
**6.1**

ANALYZE → REGRESSION → LINEAR

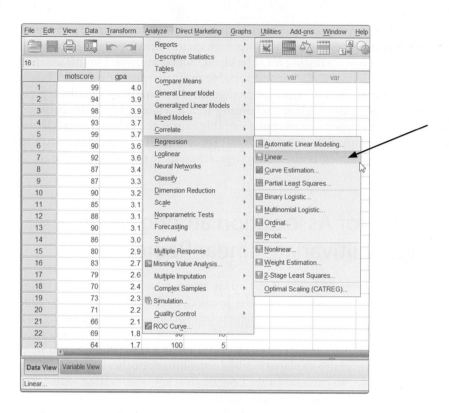

In the *Linear Regression* pop-up window, highlight *gpa* and click the arrow pointing to the *Dependent* box, and highlight *motscore*, *IQ*, and *hrsstudy* and click the arrow pointing to the *Independent(s)* box, then click **OK** as everything is set by default.

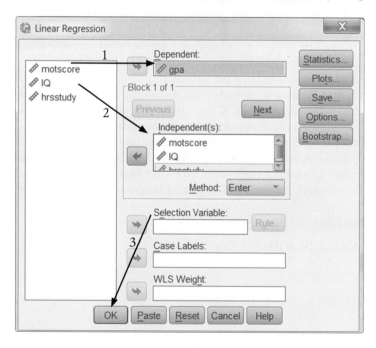

The standard Linear Regression command in IBM SPSS Statistics software ("SPSS") produces the four tables in the order seen below.

## Regression

**Variables Entered/Removed[a]**

| Model | Variables Entered | Variables Removed | Method |
|---|---|---|---|
| 1 | hrsstudy, IQ, motscore[b] | . | Enter |

a. Dependent Variable: gpa

b. All requested variables entered.

**Model Summary[b]**

| Model | R | R Square | Adjusted R Square | Std. Error of the Estimate |
|---|---|---|---|---|
| 1 | .768[a] | .589 | .559 | .4723 |

a. Predictors: (Constant), hrsstudy, IQ, motscore

b. Dependent Variable: gpa

**ANOVA[a]**

| Model | | Sum of Squares | df | Mean Square | F | Sig. |
|---|---|---|---|---|---|---|
| 1 | Regression | 13.130 | 3 | 4.377 | 19.618 | .000[b] |
| | Residual | 9.147 | 41 | .223 | | |
| | Total | 22.276 | 44 | | | |

a. Dependent Variable: gpa

b. Predictors: (Constant), hrsstudy, IQ, motscore

**Coefficients[a]**

| Model | | Unstandardized Coefficients | | Standardized Coefficients | t | Sig. |
|---|---|---|---|---|---|---|
| | | B | Std. Error | Beta | | |
| 1 | (Constant) | −1.058 | .627 | | −1.688 | .099 |
| | motscore | .023 | .004 | .554 | 5.134 | .000 |
| | IQ | .020 | .006 | .373 | 3.464 | .001 |
| | hrsstudy | .008 | .016 | .053 | .522 | .605 |

a. Dependent Variable: gpa

The first table, *Variables Entered/Removed*, as repeated below, confirms that we entered in *motscore*, *IQ*, and *hrsstudy*, all at once, as predictor variables in the model (Method = Enter), and *GPA* as the dependent variable.

**Variables Entered/Removed**[a]

| Model | Variables Entered | Variables Removed | Method |
|-------|-------------------|-------------------|--------|
| 1 | hrsstudy, IQ, motscoreb | . | Enter |

a. Dependent Variable: gpa

b. All requested variables entered.

The second table shows that all three of these independent variables collectively explain the 58.9% of the variability in GPA scores (as can be seen by the *R Square* value converted to a percentage, highlighted in the table below). We convert this proportion to a percentage to understand how large of an effect the independent variables collectively have on GPA. According to Cohen (1988), this *R squared* value (.589) shows a moderate to strong effect size for the combined effects of these variables on GPA.

**Model Summary**[b]

| Model | R | R Square | Adjusted R Square | Std. Error of the Estimate |
|-------|------|----------|-------------------|----------------------------|
| 1 | .768[a] | .589 | .559 | .4723 |

a. Predictors: (Constant), hrsstudy, IQ, motscore

b. Dependent Variable: gpa

We can also see that, together, these three predictor variables have a statistically significant association with GPA by looking at the third table below, titled *ANOVA*. Specifically, the *F* value and the *p* value (listed under *Sig*) in this table (highlighted below) tell us that collectively, motivation, IQ, and hours studied are significantly associated with GPA ($p < .001$). Another way to think about this is that motivation, IQ, and hours studied together explain a statistically significant proportion of the variability in GPA.

**ANOVA**[a]

| Model | | Sum of Squares | df | Mean Square | F | Sig. |
|-------|------------|----------------|----|-------------|--------|-------|
| 1 | Regression | 13.130 | 3 | 4.377 | 19.618 | .000[b] |
| | Residual | 9.147 | 41 | .223 | | |
| | Total | 22.276 | 44 | | | |

a. Dependent Variable: gpa

b. Predictors: (Constant), hrsstudy, IQ, motscore

Finally, the fourth table, titled *Coefficients*, tells us if each predictor variable separately predicts GPA. The *Unstandardized Coefficients B* tells us the value of the slope with the accompanying standard error (*Std. Error*), the *Beta* value tells us the slope in standardized format, and the *Sig* tells us the statistical significance (*p* value) for each predictor variable based on the *t* value listed (highlighted in the table below). When the *p* value (*Sig*) is less than or equal to .05, we would say that the variable significantly predicts GPA. In these data, we see that both motivation ($p < .001$) and IQ ($p = .001$) significantly predict GPA, but hours studied does not ($p = .605$, which shows $p > .05$, so not statistically significant). We can tell from these results that collectively these three predictor variables explain a significant amount of variability in GPA, and individually, because the slope values are positive, motivation and IQ significantly predict GPA (as motivation and IQ increase, so does GPA).

**Coefficients**[a]

| Model | | Unstandardized Coefficients | | Standardized Coefficients | | |
|---|---|---|---|---|---|---|
| | | B | Std. Error | Beta | t | Sig. |
| 1 | (Constant) | −1.058 | .627 | | −1.688 | .099 |
| | motscore | .023 | .004 | .554 | 5.134 | .000 |
| | IQ | .020 | .006 | .373 | 3.464 | .001 |
| | hrsstudy | .008 | .016 | .053 | .522 | .605 |

a. Dependent Variable: gpa

In order to write this result in APA style, we will need several pieces of information. First, we need the value and significance test information for the *R squared*, including the $R^2$ value, the *F* value, the degrees of freedom, and *p* value from the *ANOVA* table. Second, we will need the test information for each predictor variable separately, including the unstandardized coefficients (*B*), the standard error of the coefficients (*Std. Error*), the standardized coefficients (*Beta*), the *t* value, and the *p* value (*Sig.*) for each variable from the *Coefficients* table. This is what your APA-style Results section would look like for this finding:

> We hypothesized that student motivation, IQ, and hours spent studying would all be positively associated with grade point average (GPA). Collectively, these three variables explained 59% of the variance in GPA, $F(3, 41) = 19.62$, $p < .001$, $R^2 = .59$. Individual predictor variable results are reported in Table 1 showing that motivation and IQ both significantly predicted GPA in a positive direction.

*APA Style*
**6.1**

Table 1

*Summary of Regression Analysis for Prediction of GPA*

| Predictor | B | SE B | Beta | t | p |
|---|---|---|---|---|---|
| Motivation | .02 | .01 | .55 | 5.13 | < .001 |
| IQ | .02 | .01 | .37 | 3.46 | .001 |
| Hours Studied | .01 | .02 | .05 | 0.52 | .61 |

*Note:* N = 45, $R^2$ = .59.

# 6.2 Testing for Association among Multiple Variables: Hierarchical Linear Regression

When running a regression analysis, there are reasons to conduct the analysis a bit differently than simply entering in multiple predictors simultaneously (as we did in Section 6.1). Sometimes you would like to enter in some variables that are known predictors of the dependent variable first (in what we call entering in a "block"), and then see if your variable of interest predicts the dependent variable over and above the known predictors' association. This is a way to "control" for the effects of one variable first and then test the effects of another variable. If we want to enter in variables in separate blocks, then hierarchical linear regression would be appropriate. Hierarchical regression allows us to control the order of entering the variables and to see how much the variables contribute to predicting the dependent variable at each step. This is done by looking at the proportion of variance each variable explains and the change in that proportion of variance as we add another variable or set of variables in a second block. Based on previous literature, we could hypothesize that IQ is a predictor of GPA. We may also be interested in motivation and study time's additional prediction of GPA, so running a hierarchical regression would make sense in our example. Here's how to run a hierarchical regression using *GPA* as the dependent variable, with *IQ* entered first, and then *motscore* and *hrsstudy* entered second in a block.

Select from the Top Menu Bar:

*SPSS Commands 6.2*

ANALYZE → REGRESSION → LINEAR

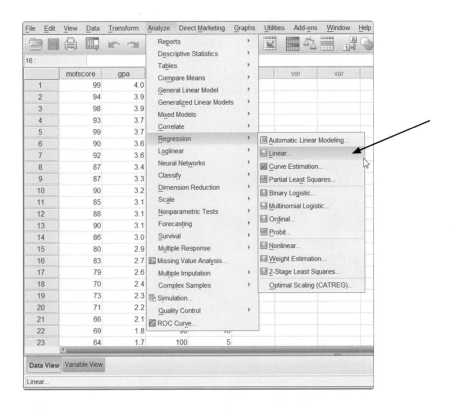

In the *Linear Regression* pop-up window, highlight *gpa* and click the arrow pointing to the *Dependent* box, and highlight *IQ* and click the arrow pointing to the *Independent(s)* box, then click the *Next* button.

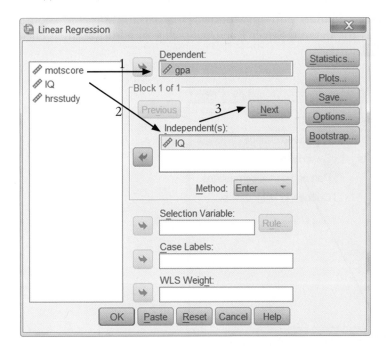

Then, highlight *motscore* and *hrsstudy* and click the arrow pointing to the *Independent(s)* box in the "Next" step, then click Statistics…. You could enter each of these two variables separately by choosing *Method: Stepwise,* but we are just using *Enter* and entering in both variables simultaneously in the second block. The stepwise process would enter the variables one at a time, but we have no theoretical reason to believe that one of the variables should be entered first, so we will enter them both simultaneously.

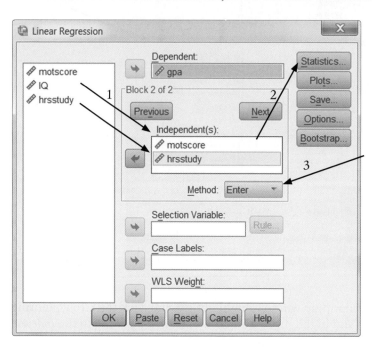

In the *Linear Regression: Statistics* pop-up window, *Estimates* and *Model fit* should be already selected as the default. Select *R squared change* in addition, then click Continue, then click OK.

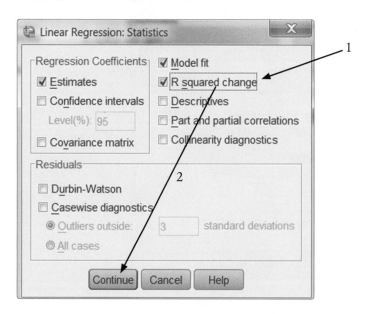

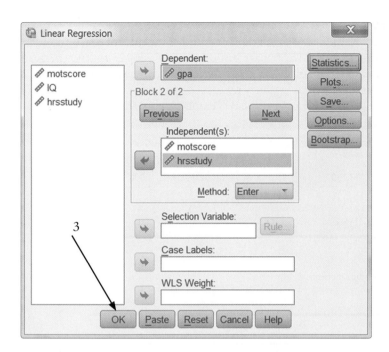

When you run this Hierarchical Regression following these commands, SPSS provides these five tables in this order:

*SPSS Output* **6.2**

## Regression

**Variables Entered/Removed[a]**

| Model | Variables Entered | Variables Removed | Method |
|-------|-------------------|-------------------|--------|
| 1 | IQ[b] | . | Enter |
| 2 | hrsstudy, motscore[b] | . | Enter |

a. Dependent Variable: gpa

b. All requested variables entered.

**Model Summary**

| Model | R | R Square | Adjusted R Square | Std. Error of the Estimate | R Square Change | F Change | df1 | df2 | Sig. F Change |
|-------|---|----------|-------------------|----------------------------|-----------------|----------|-----|-----|---------------|
| | | | | | Change Statistics | | | | |
| 1 | .570[a] | .325 | .310 | .5912 | .325 | 20.740 | 1 | 43 | .000 |
| 2 | .768[b] | .589 | .559 | .4723 | .264 | 13.181 | 2 | 41 | .000 |

a. Predictors: (Constant), IQ

b. Predictors: (Constant), IQ, hrsstudy, motscore

## ANOVA[a]

| Model | | Sum of Squares | df | Mean Square | F | Sig. |
|---|---|---|---|---|---|---|
| 1 | Regression | 7.249 | 1 | 7.249 | 20.740 | .000[b] |
| | Residual | 15.028 | 43 | .349 | | |
| | Total | 22.276 | 44 | | | |
| 2 | Regression | 13.130 | 3 | 4.377 | 19.618 | .000[c] |
| | Residual | 9.147 | 41 | .223 | | |
| | Total | 22.276 | 44 | | | |

a. Dependent Variable: gpa

b. Predictors: (Constant), IQ

c. Predictors: (Constant), IQ, hrsstudy, motscore

## Coefficients[a]

| Model | | Unstandardized Coefficients | | Standardized Coefficients | t | Sig. |
|---|---|---|---|---|---|---|
| | | B | Std. Error | Beta | | |
| 1 | (Constant) | −.264 | .715 | | −.369 | .714 |
| | IQ | .031 | .007 | .570 | 4.554 | .000 |
| 2 | (Constant) | −1.058 | .627 | | −1.688 | .099 |
| | IQ | .020 | .006 | .373 | 3.464 | .001 |
| | motscore | .023 | .004 | .554 | 5.134 | .000 |
| | hrsstudy | .008 | .016 | .053 | .522 | .605 |

a. Dependent Variable: gpa

## Excluded Variables[a]

| Model | | Beta In | t | Sig. | Partial Correlation | Collinearity Statistics |
|---|---|---|---|---|---|---|
| | | | | | | Tolerance |
| 1 | motscore | .549[b] | 5.153 | .000 | .622 | .867 |
| | hrsstudy | .002[b] | .015 | .988 | .002 | .994 |

a. Dependent Variable: gpa

b. Predictors in the Model: (Constant), IQ

The first table, *Variables Entered/Removed*, as seen below, confirms that we entered in *IQ* alone first in Model 1, and then *motscore* and *hrsstudy* together in Model 2, with *gpa* as the dependent variable.

**Variables Entered/Removed[a]**

| Model | Variables Entered | Variables Removed | Method |
|---|---|---|---|
| 1 | IQ[b] | . | Enter |
| 2 | hrsstudy, motscoreb | . | Enter |

a. Dependent Variable: gpa

b. All requested variables entered.

The second table shows how well GPA is predicted by IQ (Model 1), and how well motivation and hours studied predicts GPA over and above IQ (Model 2). IQ accounted for a significant amount of the variability in GPA (32.5%, specifically), as seen by the *R Square* value of .325 and the *p* value (*Sig. F Change*) < .001. Motivation and hours studied accounted for a significant proportion of the variability in GPA after controlling for the effects of IQ. Motivation and hours studied explained an additional 26.4% of the variability in GPA over and above IQ (seen by the value of *R Square Change* for Model 2). This was a significant increase in prediction of GPA with these two additional variables, as seen by the *p* value (*Sig. F Change*) < .001. The *R Square Change* and *Sig. F Change* values show how much the F statistic and the *p* value changed when the second block was entered.

**Model Summary**

| Model | R | R Square | Adjusted R Square | Std. Error of the Estimate | Change Statistics | | | | |
|---|---|---|---|---|---|---|---|---|---|
| | | | | | R Square Change | F Change | df1 | df2 | Sig. F Change |
| 1 | .570[a] | .325 | .310 | .5912 | .325 | 20.740 | 1 | 43 | .000 |
| 2 | .768[b] | .589 | .559 | .4723 | .264 | 13.181 | 2 | 41 | .000 |

a. Predictors: (Constant), IQ

b. Predictors: (Constant), IQ, hrsstudy, motscore

Skipping to the fourth table titled *Coefficients*, we can assess if each independent variable separately predicts GPA. The *Unstandardized Coefficients B* for each variable tells us the value of the slope for that independent variable, and the *Sig* tells us the statistical significance (*p* value) of each, highlighted in the table below. In this data, we see that both IQ (*p* = .001) and motivation (*p* < .001) significantly predict GPA, but hours studied does not (*p* = .605, showing that *p* > .05, so not statistically significant). We can tell from these results that motivation significantly and positively predicts GPA, controlling for IQ. In other words, IQ predicts quite a bit of the variance in GPA, but motivation adds to that.

**Coefficients[a]**

| Model | | Unstandardized Coefficients | | Standardized Coefficients | | |
|---|---|---|---|---|---|---|
| | | B | Std. Error | Beta | t | Sig. |
| 1 | (Constant) | −.264 | .715 | | −.369 | .714 |
| | IQ | .031 | .007 | .570 | 4.554 | .000 |
| 2 | (Constant) | −1.058 | .627 | | −1.688 | .099 |
| | IQ | .020 | .006 | .373 | 3.464 | .001 |
| | motscore | .023 | .004 | .554 | 5.134 | .000 |
| | hrsstudy | .008 | .016 | .053 | .522 | .605 |

a. Dependent Variable: gpa

*APA Style*
*6.2*

In order to write this result in APA style, we will need several pieces of information. First, we need the value and significance test information for the *R square* change, the *F* change value, the degrees of freedom, and *p* values (*Sig. F Change*) from the *ANOVA* table. Second, we will need the test information for each independent variable separately, including the standardized coefficient (*Beta*) and *p* value for each variable from the *Coefficients* table. This is what your APA-style Results section would look like for this finding:

A hierarchical multiple regression analysis was conducted to predict grade point average (GPA) from IQ, motivation to succeed in life, and hours spent studying per week. The results of the first step of this analysis showed that IQ accounted for a significant amount of GPA variability, $R^2 = .33$, $F(1, 43) = 20.74$, $p < .001$, indicating that students with higher IQ values tended to have higher GPA values.

A second step was conducted to evaluate whether motivation and hours studied predicted GPA over and above IQ. Motivation and hours studied accounted for a significant proportion of the GPA variance after controlling for the effects of IQ, $R^2$ change $= .26$, $F(2, 41) = 13.18$, $p < .001$. Specifically, only motivation significantly predicted GPA ($\beta = .55$, $p < .001$) over and above IQ's significant unique prediction ($\beta = .37$, $p = .001$).

# 6.3 Using Regression to Test for Mediation

Oftentimes, when we find a significant association between a predictor variable and a dependent variable, we want to explore it further and find out why the relationship exists. This may lead us to another type of relationship, called *mediation*. Rather than hypothesizing a direct relationship between the independent variable and the dependent variable, a mediational model hypothesizes that the independent variable influences the mediator variable, which in turn influences the dependent variable. For this example, we will use the relationship between motivation and GPA, but consider the mediating effect of a third variable, positive teacher perception (called *PosTeachPerc*). Positive teacher perception data was also collected on the 45 students in my research methods class, along with motivation and GPA. Positive teacher perception is a variable that rates teacher feedback as being low, moderate, or high on the positive scale, with high being the most positive teacher feedback and low being the least positive teacher feedback. If a student believed that the teacher's feedback was very positive, then *PosTeachPerc* would be high, and if the student believed that the teacher's feedback was not at all positive, then *PosTeachPerc* would be low. When entering in *PosTeachPerc*, a value of 1 was entered for "low," 2 for "moderate," and 3 for "high" levels of positive teacher perceptions. We hypothesized that how students perceived the teacher's feedback would mediate the relationship between their motivation and GPA. In other words, motivation would be positively associated with their rating of positive teacher feedback (*PosTeachPerc*), which would, in turn, be positively associated with GPA. This is what the data look like:

| File | Edit | View | Data | Transform | Analyze | Direct |
|------|------|------|------|-----------|---------|--------|

| 19 : | | | |
|---|---|---|---|
| | PosTeachPerc | motscore | gpa |
| 1 | 3 | 99 | 4.0 |
| 2 | 2 | 94 | 3.9 |
| 3 | 3 | 98 | 3.9 |
| 4 | 3 | 93 | 3.7 |
| 5 | 3 | 99 | 3.7 |
| 6 | 2 | 90 | 3.6 |
| 7 | 2 | 92 | 3.6 |
| 8 | 3 | 87 | 3.4 |
| 9 | 3 | 87 | 3.3 |
| 10 | 3 | 90 | 3.2 |
| 11 | 2 | 85 | 3.1 |
| 12 | 3 | 88 | 3.1 |
| 13 | 3 | 90 | 3.1 |
| 14 | 1 | 86 | 3.0 |
| 15 | 2 | 80 | 2.9 |
| 16 | 3 | 83 | 2.7 |
| 17 | 2 | 79 | 2.6 |
| 18 | 2 | 70 | 2.4 |
| 19 | 1 | 73 | 2.3 |
| 20 | 2 | 71 | 2.2 |
| 21 | 2 | 66 | 2.1 |
| 22 | 1 | 69 | 1.8 |

Data View | Variable View

It is often helpful to draw a diagram of the mediation model you are hypothesizing to keep your variables and associations straight. Here is the diagram of the mediation model of positive teacher perception mediating the relationship between motivation and GPA. In the analysis, we would expect that there would be a significant relationship between the independent variable (motivation) and the dependent variable (GPA) (labeled as arrow *c*), but a non-significant relationship when the mediator (positive teacher perception) is also in the model.

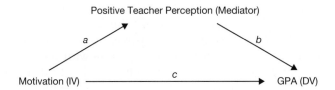

Testing mediation using linear regression is a four-step process. We will use the diagram above to refer to different associations that we will test between the independent variable (motivation), the mediator (positive teacher perception), and the dependent variable (GPA).

Here are the four steps we will follow:

1. We will test association *c* between motivation and GPA.

2. We will test association *a* between motivation and positive teacher perception.

3. We will test association *b* between positive teacher perception and GPA.

4. We will test association *c*, again, between motivation and GPA, but also include positive teacher perception in the model.

If positive teacher perception is a mediator of the relationship between motivation and GPA, we would expect steps 1 through 3 to show significant associations, but not the relationship between motivation and GPA in step 4, with positive teacher perception also in the model.

*SPSS Commands*
**6.3**

You will have four different regression results, and it is important to keep them all separate and organized to understand if positive teacher perception is a mediator. For all four steps, you will run a linear regression analysis using this command to get the *Linear Regression* pop-up window in SPSS.

Select from the Top Menu Bar:

ANALYZE → REGRESSION → LINEAR

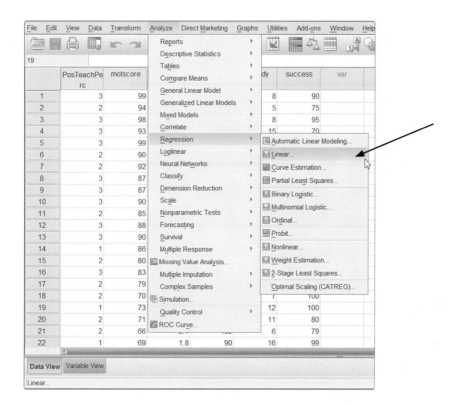

## STEP 1: Association *c*. Motivation Predicting GPA

In the *Linear Regression* pop-up window, highlight *gpa* and click the arrow pointing to the *Dependent* box, and highlight *motscore* and click the arrow pointing to the *Independent(s)* box, then click **OK**.

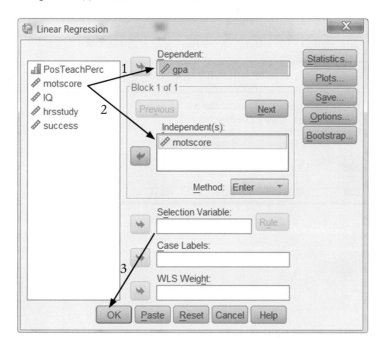

This is the output for Step 1.

## Regression

### Variables Entered/Removed[a]

| Model | Variables Entered | Variables Removed | Method |
|-------|-------------------|-------------------|--------|
| 1 | motscore[b] | . | Enter |

a. Dependent Variable: gpa

b. All requested variables entered.

### Model Summary

| Model | R | R Square | Adjusted R Square | Std. Error of the Estimate |
|-------|------|----------|-------------------|----------------------------|
| 1 | .684[a] | .468 | .455 | .5251 |

a. Predictors: (Constant), motscore

### ANOVA[a]

| Model | | Sum of Squares | df | Mean Square | F | Sig. |
|-------|------------|----------------|----|-------------|--------|-------|
| 1 | Regression | 10.419 | 1 | 10.419 | 37.785 | .000[b] |
| | Residual | 11.857 | 43 | .276 | | |
| | Total | 22.276 | 44 | | | |

a. Dependent Variable: gpa

b. Predictors: (Constant), motscore

### Coefficients[a]

| Model | | Unstandardized Coefficients | | Standardized Coefficients | t | Sig. |
|-------|------------|------|-----------|------|-------|------|
| | | B | Std. Error | Beta | | |
| 1 | (Constant) | .710 | .376 | | 1.889 | .066 |
| | motscore | .028 | .005 | .684 | 6.147 | .000 |

a. Dependent Variable: gpa

## STEP 2: Association *a*. Motivation Predicting Positive Teacher Perception

In the *Linear Regression* pop-up window, highlight *PosTeachPerc* and click the arrow pointing to the *Dependent* box, and highlight *motscore* and click the arrow pointing to the *Independent(s)* box, then click **OK**.

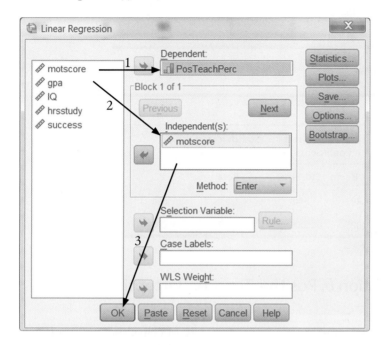

This is the output for Step 2.

## Regression

### Variables Entered/Removed[a]

| Model | Variables Entered | Variables Removed | Method |
| --- | --- | --- | --- |
| 1 | motscore[b] | . | Enter |

a. Dependent Variable: PosTeachPerc

b. All requested variables entered.

### Model Summary

| Model | R | R Square | Adjusted R Square | Std. Error of the Estimate |
| --- | --- | --- | --- | --- |
| 1 | .566[a] | .321 | .305 | .626 |

a. Predictors: (Constant), motscore

**ANOVA**[a]

| Model | | Sum of Squares | df | Mean Square | F | Sig. |
|---|---|---|---|---|---|---|
| 1 | Regression | 7.955 | 1 | 7.955 | 20.307 | .000[b] |
| | Residual | 16.845 | 43 | .392 | | |
| | Total | 24.800 | 44 | | | |

a. Dependent Variable: PosTeachPerc

b. Predictors: (Constant), motscore

**Coefficients**[a]

| Model | | Unstandardized Coefficients | | Standardized Coefficients | t | Sig. |
|---|---|---|---|---|---|---|
| | | B | Std. Error | Beta | | |
| 1 | (Constant) | .293 | .448 | | .654 | .517 |
| | motscore | .025 | .006 | .566 | 4.506 | .000 |

a. Dependent Variable: PosTeachPerc

## STEP 3: Association *b*. Positive Teacher Perception Predicting GPA

In the *Linear Regression* pop-up window, highlight *gpa* and click the arrow pointing to the *Dependent* box, and highlight *PosTeachPerc* and click the arrow pointing to the *Independent(s)* box, then click **OK**.

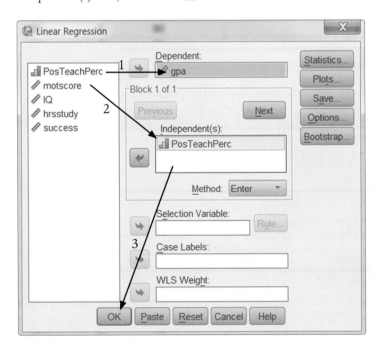

This is the output for Step 3.

## Regression

### Variables Entered/Removed[a]

| Model | Variables Entered | Variables Removed | Method |
|-------|-------------------|-------------------|--------|
| 1 | PosTeachPerc[b] | . | Enter |

a. Dependent Variable: gpa

b. All requested variables entered.

### Model Summary

| Model | R | R Square | Adjusted R Square | Std. Error of the Estimate |
|-------|-----|----------|-------------------|----------------------------|
| 1 | .650[a] | .422 | .409 | .5471 |

a. Predictors: (Constant), PosTeachPerc

### ANOVA[a]

| Model | | Sum of Squares | df | Mean Square | F | Sig. |
|-------|------------|----------------|----|-------------|--------|-------|
| 1 | Regression | 9.406 | 1 | 9.406 | 31.427 | .000[b] |
| | Residual | 12.870 | 43 | .299 | | |
| | Total | 22.276 | 44 | | | |

a. Dependent Variable: gpa

b. Predictors: (Constant), PosTeachPerc

### Coefficients[a]

| Model | | Unstandardized Coefficients | | Standardized Coefficients | t | Sig. |
|-------|--------------|------|------------|------|-------|------|
| | | B | Std. Error | Beta | | |
| 1 | (Constant) | 1.573 | .262 | | 6.003 | .000 |
| | PosTeachPerc | .616 | .110 | .650 | 5.606 | .000 |

a. Dependent Variable: gpa

## STEP 4: Association *c* Again. Motivation and Positive Teacher Perception Predicting GPA

We now return to the relationship between motivation and GPA, but also add in positive teacher perception. In a classic mediation model, if motivation's association with GPA is reduced to a non-significant relationship, then positive teacher perception would be a mediator in the relationship between motivation and GPA. In the *Linear Regression* pop-up window, highlight *gpa* and click on the arrow pointing to the *Dependent* box, and highlight *motscore* and *PosTeachPerc* and click on the arrow pointing to the *Independent(s)* box, then click **OK**.

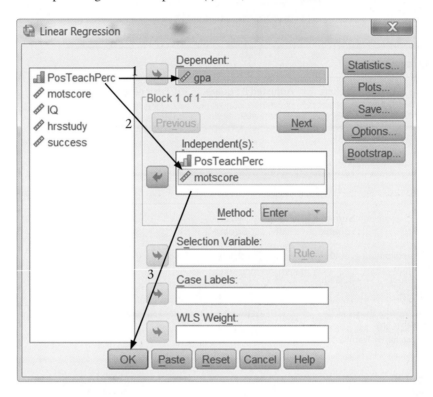

This is the output for Step 4.

## Regression

**Variables Entered/Removed[a]**

| Model | Variables Entered | Variables Removed | Method |
|---|---|---|---|
| 1 | PosTeachPerc, motscore[b] | . | Enter |

a. Dependent Variable: gpa

b. All requested variables entered.

## Model Summary

| Model | R | R Square | Adjusted R Square | Std. Error of the Estimate |
|---|---|---|---|---|
| 1 | .754[a] | .569 | .549 | .4780 |

a. Predictors: (Constant), PosTeachPerc, motscore

## ANOVA[a]

| Model | | Sum of Squares | df | Mean Square | F | Sig. |
|---|---|---|---|---|---|---|
| 1 | Regression | 12.679 | 2 | 6.339 | 27.741 | .000[b] |
| | Residual | 9.598 | 42 | .229 | | |
| | Total | 22.276 | 44 | | | |

a. Dependent Variable: gpa

b. Predictors: (Constant), PosTeachPerc, motscore

## Coefficients[a]

| Model | | Unstandardized Coefficients | | Standardized Coefficients | t | Sig. |
|---|---|---|---|---|---|---|
| | | B | Std. Error | Beta | | |
| 1 | (Constant) | .603 | .344 | | 1.753 | .087 |
| | motscore | .019 | .005 | .465 | 3.784 | .000 |
| | PosTeachPerc | .366 | .116 | .386 | 3.144 | .003 |

a. Dependent Variable: gpa

*Interpretation 6.3*

You will have four different regression results, and it is important to have them organized to understand if positive teacher perception is a mediator. We will need two pieces of information from the *Coefficients* table from each of the four regression outputs: the β value (found under *Standardized Coefficients Beta*), and *p* value (*Sig.*) for each of the relationships listed in the four steps.

1. Association *c* between motivation and GPA is significant ($\beta = .68, p < .001$).

2. Association *a* between motivation and positive teacher perception is significant ($\beta = .57, p < .001$).

3. Association *b* between positive teacher perception and GPA is significant ($\beta = .65, p < .001$).

4. Association *c*, again, between motivation and GPA that also includes positive teacher perception in the model. If positive teacher perception is a mediator, then we would expect motivation's association with GPA to

be reduced to a non-significant relationship when positive teacher perception is also in the model. Unfortunately, this is not the case. Motivation still has a significant association with GPA ($\beta$ = .47, $p$ < .001) when positive teacher perception is included in the analysis showing that it is not a mediating variable.

It is easiest to note these values using the diagram and inserting the $\beta$ values, using asterisks to denote significance values.

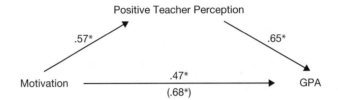

**FIGURE 1** Total and direct effects of motivation on GPA

*Total effect in parentheses; *p < .001.*

Our hypothesis of mediation was not supported, as motivation still had a significant association with GPA even when positive teacher perception was in the model. Therefore, there is no reason to write up this result in APA style. For a great example of a mediation hypothesis that is supported and reported in APA style, see Drouin (2014).

## 6.4 Using Correlation to Test for Moderation

Moderation is another possibility when considering relationships among variables. Moderation is when the relationship between the independent and dependent variable changes depending on the levels of a third variable, called a *moderator*. In other words, when the moderator variable is high in value, we expect the association between the two other variables to be different from the association when the moderator is low. We may hypothesize that motivation's relationship with GPA may be moderated depending on level of positive teacher perception. For example, we hypothesize that the relationship between motivation and GPA will be strongly positive when positive teacher perception is high, but not as strongly positive when positive teacher perception is low. To test this, we would assess separately the association (correlation) between motivation and GPA for each of the three levels of positive teacher perception. To accomplish this, we would need to select the data for one level of *PosTeachPerc* at a time, and then run a correlation analysis for each level.

To select each level of positive teacher perception, select from the Top Menu Bar:

DATA → SELECT CASES

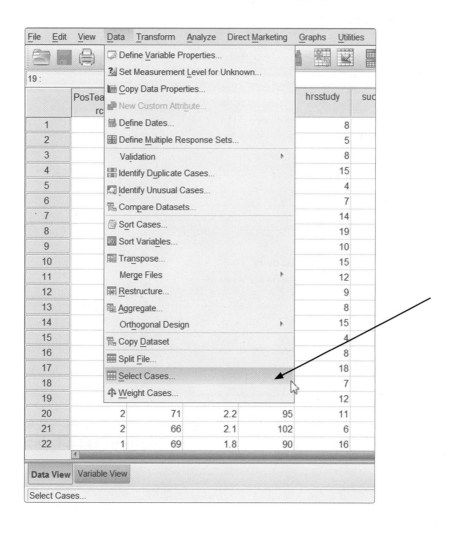

In the *Select Cases* pop-up window, click on the small circle that says *If condition is satisfied*, then click on the **If...** button.

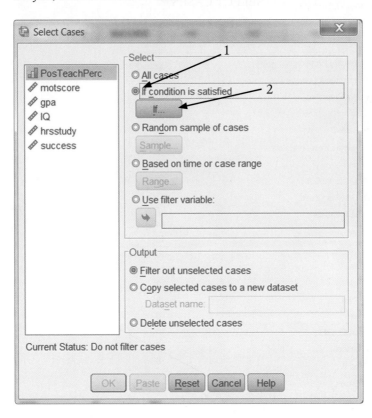

In the *Select Cases: If* pop-up window, highlight *PosTeachPerc* and click on the arrow pointing to the blank box, then type = 1 (for the low level), then click **Continue**, then click **OK**.

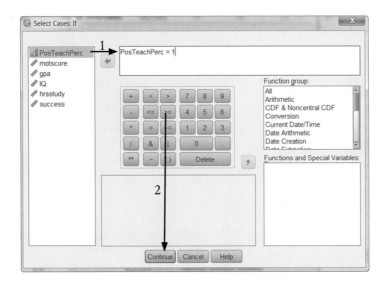

To run the correlation between motivation and GPA for just the low level of positive teacher perception, do this after you select *PosTeachPerc = 1*.

Select from the Top Menu Bar:

ANALYZE → CORRELATE → BIVARIATE

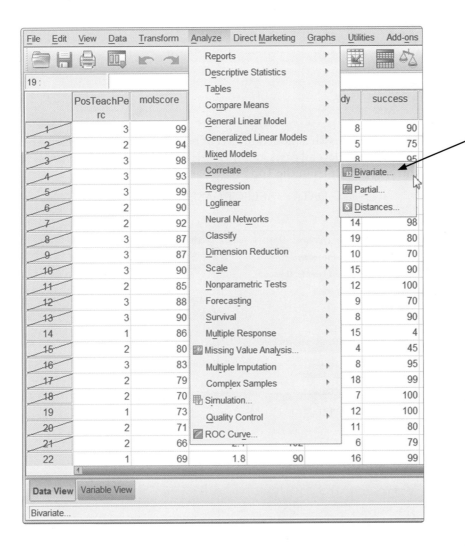

Note that all of the *PosTeachPerc* values that are not 1 are crossed off for this analysis because we are only concentrating on the low level = 1.

In the *Bivariate Correlations* pop-up window, highlight *motscore* and *gpa* and click on the arrow pointing to the *Variables* box, then click **OK**.

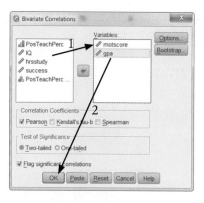

Now, to replicate this process at a moderate level of positive teacher perception, you will have to go back and select all cases and then select *PosTeachPerc = 2*.

To select all cases, select from the Top Menu Bar:

DATA → SELECT CASES

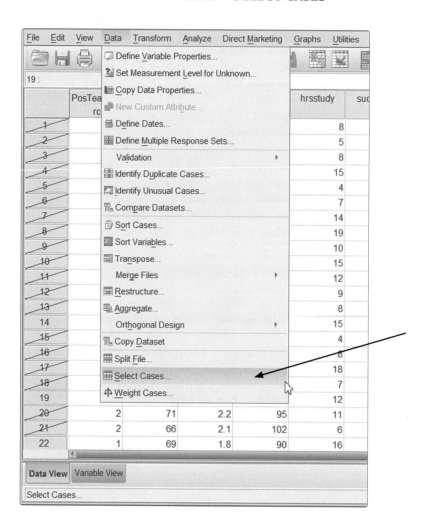

In the *Select Cases* pop-up window, click on the small circle that says *All cases*, then click OK.

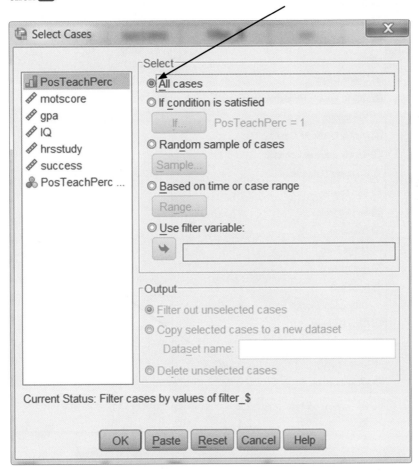

Now, to select the moderate level (= 2) of positive teacher perception, select from the Top Menu Bar:

DATA → SELECT CASES

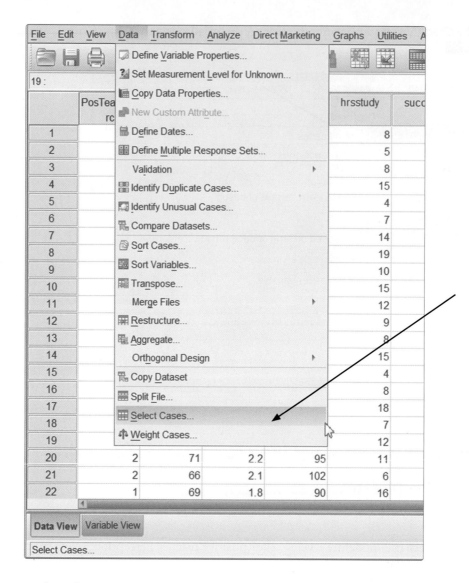

In the *Select Cases* pop-up window, click on the small circle that says *If condition is satisfied*, then click on the **If...** button.

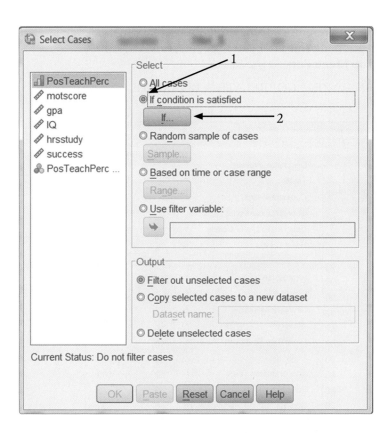

In the *Select Cases: If* pop-up window, highlight *PosTeachPerc* and click the arrow pointing to the blank box, and then type = 2 (for the moderate level), then click **Continue**, then click **OK**.

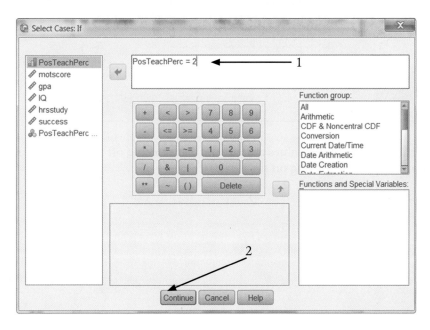

To run the correlation between motivation and GPA for just the moderate level of positive teacher perception, do this after you select *PosTeachPerc = 2*.

Select from the Top Menu Bar:

ANALYZE → CORRELATE → BIVARIATE

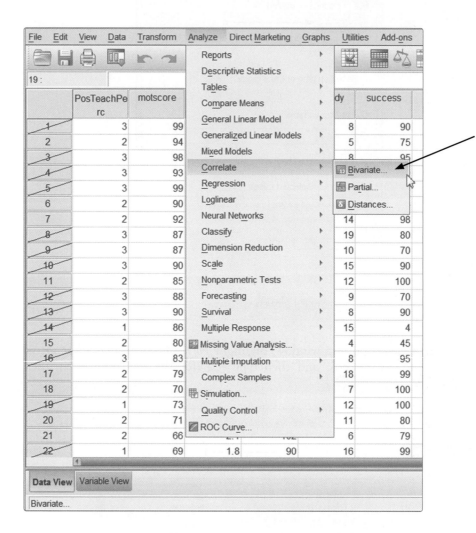

Note that all of the *PosTeachPerc* values that are not 2 are crossed off for this analysis because we are only concentrating on the moderate level = 2.

In the *Bivariate Correlations* pop-up window, highlight *motscore* and *gpa* and click the arrow pointing to the *Variables* box, then click **OK**.

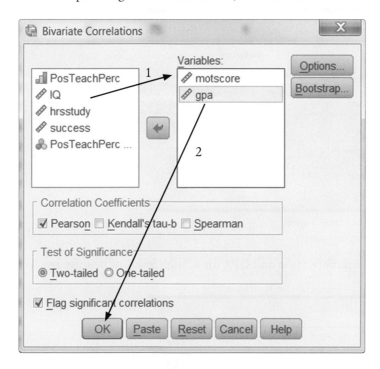

Now, go back and *Select All* cases like you just did for the moderate level, then *Select cases If PosTeachPerc = 3* for the high level, and run that correlation analysis just the same as above.

When you run a correlation at each level of *PosTeachPerc* separately, SPSS provides the following three correlation outputs.

SPSS Output 6.4

The correlation between motivation and GPA for a "low" level of positive teacher perception:

## Correlations

|          |                     | motscore | gpa    |
|----------|---------------------|----------|--------|
| motscore | Pearson Correlation | 1        | −.040  |
|          | Sig. (2-tailed)     |          | .925   |
|          | N                   | 8        | 8      |
| gpa      | Pearson Correlation | −.040    | 1      |
|          | Sig. (2-tailed)     | .925     |        |
|          | N                   | 8        | 8      |

The correlation between motivation and GPA for a "moderate" level of positive teacher perception:

## Correlations

|  |  | motscore | gpa |
|---|---|---|---|
| motscore | Pearson Correlation | 1 | .805** |
|  | Sig. (2-tailed) |  | .000 |
|  | N | 17 | 17 |
| gpa | Pearson Correlation | .805** | 1 |
|  | Sig. (2-tailed) | .000 |  |
|  | N | 17 | 17 |

**Correlation is significant at the .01 level (2-tailed).

The correlation between motivation and GPA for a "high level" of positive teacher perception:

## Correlations

|  |  | motscore | gpa |
|---|---|---|---|
| motscore | Pearson Correlation | 1 | .493* |
|  | Sig. (2-tailed) |  | .027 |
|  | N | 20 | 20 |
| gpa | Pearson Correlation | .493* | 1 |
|  | Sig. (2-tailed) | .027 |  |
|  | N | 20 | 20 |

*Correlation is significant at the .05 level (2-tailed).

*Interpretation 6.4*

The three correlation values tell us that the relationship between motivation and GPA is moderated by level of positive teacher perception. We can tell this because the correlation is only significant at two of the three levels of positive teacher perception. Positive teacher perception moderates the relationship between motivation and GPA significantly at the moderate and high levels (low level: $r = -.04$, *ns*; moderate level: $r = .81$, $p < .001$; high level: $r = .49$, $p = .03$).

APA Style
6.4

For reporting in APA style, we only need the correlation values and the corresponding significance levels. A table like Table 1 below shows the moderation well.

Positive teacher perception had a moderating effect on the relationship between student's motivation to succeed and grade point average (GPA). At both moderate and high levels of positive teacher perception motivation was positively related to GPA, but at a low level of positive teacher perception the relationship between motivation and GPA was not significant. Correlations at each level of positive teacher perception are reported in Table 2.

Table 2

*Positive Teacher Perception Moderates the Relationship Between Motivation and GPA*

| Level of Positive Teacher Perception | Association (r) between motivation and GPA |
|---|---|
| Low | −.05 |
| Moderate | .81** |
| High | .49* |

*$p < .05$
**$p < .001$

## References

Cohen, J. (1988). *Statistical power analysis for the behavioral sciences* (2nd ed.). Hillsdale, NJ: Erlbaum.

Drouin, M. A. (2014). If you record it, some won't come: Using lecture capture in Introductory Psychology. *Teaching of Psychology 41*(1), 11-19. doi: 10.1177/0098628313514172

# 7

# Analyzing Data with Nonparametric Statistics

*Many research projects use data that cannot be analyzed using the statistics we've covered so far because the data fail to meet the assumptions of the parametric test. In this chapter, you will learn how to use a range of common nonparametric statistics that could be used when your data do not meet parametric assumptions.*

## Before We Get Started: Why Use Nonparametric Statistics?

Sometimes when we collect data for a class or other smaller-scale project, our data fail to meet some of the basic assumptions needed to use inferential statistics. One of the most typical situations is having a sample size less than 25, leading to the frequent violation of the normality assumption. In these situations, it may be better to use a type of statistic, called a *nonparametric statistic*, to answer your research question. Nonparametric statistics, such as the ones covered in this chapter, tend to be more robust—they will allow you to violate some of the assumptions needed for parametric statistics and still be a reliable indicator of your findings. Typically, these nonparametric tests mirror a parametric test in the type of question it will address. In this chapter, we will cover some of the most commonly used nonparametric statistics.

# 7.1 Spearman's Rho as a Measure of Association between Two Variables

If you want to test an association between two variables, but those variables do not meet the general assumptions of the Pearson correlation test covered in Chapter 3, Section 2 (e.g., the variables are not normally distributed, the variables are ordinal, or you have outliers), then the Spearman's correlation is a good choice to test your hypothesis. Spearman's Rho allows you to test for an association between two variables that are not normally distributed, because it uses the ranks of the variables to compute the correlation coefficient.

---

**THE DATA** ────────────────────────────────────────────────

For this Spearman's correlation test, we will use data from a study conducted by my research methods class. Students were interested in studying the relationship between hours of video games played per week and GPA. They asked the following two questions of 20 participants:

1. **How many hours in an average week during the semester do you play video games of any type?** _____ **hours**
2. **What is your cumulative GPA to the nearest tenth (e.g., 2.9)?** _____._____

---

However, when students collected their data they found that, of the 20 people in their sample, two people reported hours of video gaming that were far afield from the rest of their data. They treated these two responses as outliers because these responses were nearly three standard deviations away from the mean number of hours of gaming. Because these data did not meet the assumptions of the parametric statistic, the Pearson correlation would not be appropriate. Therefore, we will use the Spearman's Rho test to answer the question of whether there is a significant relationship between hours of video gaming (named *hrsgaming*) and GPA (named *GPA*) using the following IBM SPSS Statistics software ("SPSS") commands.

Here are what the data look like in Data View (note that you have to leave the decimal places at 1 for GPA to make sure you have GPA listed to the tenth):

| | hrsgaming | GPA |
|---|---|---|
| 1 | 14 | 3.2 |
| 2 | 7 | 2.8 |
| 3 | 0 | 3.8 |
| 4 | 7 | 3.0 |
| 5 | 14 | 2.9 |
| 6 | 14 | 2.5 |
| 7 | 21 | 2.7 |
| 8 | 14 | 3.0 |
| 9 | 21 | 2.4 |
| 10 | 60 | 2.9 |
| 11 | 0 | 3.7 |
| 12 | 14 | 2.0 |
| 13 | 18 | 2.9 |
| 14 | 20 | 2.6 |
| 15 | 70 | 3.0 |
| 16 | 25 | 3.0 |
| 17 | 10 | 3.2 |
| 18 | 5 | 3.0 |
| 19 | 7 | 3.6 |
| 20 | 0 | 3.8 |
| 21 | | |
| 22 | | |
| 23 | | |

File   Edit   View   Data   Transform

Data View   Variable View

Select from the Top Menu Bar:

ANALYZE → CORRELATE → BIVARIATE

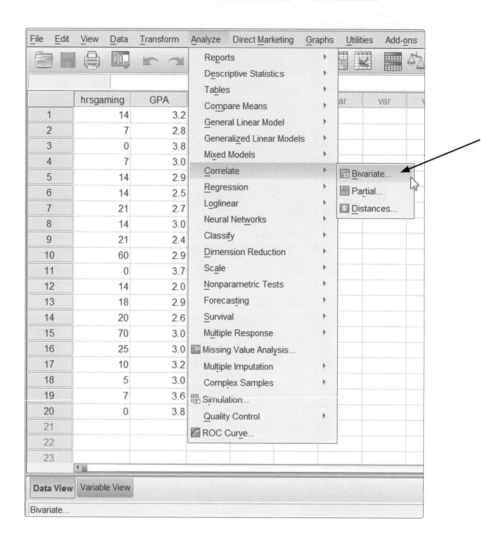

In the *Bivariate Correlations* pop-up window, double-click the two variables you want to test and they will appear in the *Variables:* box like I did with *hrsgaming* and *GPA*, then check *Spearman*, then click **OK**. Note that Pearson is checked by default, and you can choose to uncheck that or leave it as I did here.

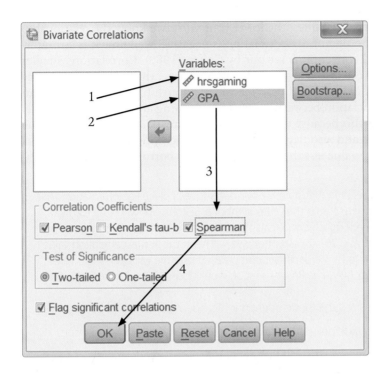

SPSS Output
7.1

When you run this analysis, SPSS gives you the following nonparametric correlation output.

## Nonparametric Correlations

**Correlations**

| | | | hrsgaming | GPA |
|---|---|---|---|---|
| Spearman's rho | hrsgaming | Correlation Coefficient | 1.000 | −.582** |
| | | Sig. (2-tailed) | . | .007 |
| | | N | 20 | 20 |
| | GPA | Correlation Coefficient | −.582** | 1.000 |
| | | Sig. (2-tailed) | .007 | . |
| | | N | 20 | 20 |

**Correlation is significant at the 0.01 level (2-tailed)

Interpretation
7.1

Much like a Pearson correlation, the Spearman's Rho describes both the direction and the strength of the relationship between *hrsgaming* and *GPA*, as well as whether that association is statistically significant. SPSS gives you the correlation in matrix format, where the same information is shown twice, once in the lower left and then mirrored in the upper right. The first line in the cell shows the Spearmen correlation between *hrsgaming* and *GPA*: −.58 (highlighted above). We can interpret that by saying there is a negative and moderate association between *hrsgaming* and *GPA*—the more hours you play video games, the lower your GPA. We know the relationship is negative because the sign of the correlation is negative. We know it is strong by following the general conventions set out by Cohen (1988). Correlations smaller than .3 are weak, between .3 and .6 are moderate, and larger than .6 are strong. Since −.58 is slightly below .6, we would describe the relationship as moderate. We can also tell that the association between hours spent gaming and GPA is statistically significant. We know this because the $p$ value is less than .05. SPSS lists the $p$ value (in this case, $p$ = .007) and also flags this significant correlation with two asterisks that correspond to a $p$ value less than .01, shown at the bottom of the table.

<table>
<tr><td>

*APA Style*
**7.1**

</td><td>

In order to write this result in APA style, we will need several pieces of information. First, the symbol for Spearman's Rho is the Greek symbol ρ. Second, we will need to calculate the degrees of freedom, which are calculated by the sample size ($N$ on the output) minus two; so, in this case: 20 − 2 = 18. Then, we will need the actual correlation value rounded to two places past the decimal point (−.58). Finally, we will need the $p$ value (.007). This is what your APA-style Results section would look like for this finding:

> We hypothesized that hours spent playing video games would be negatively associated with grade point average (GPA). The Spearman's correlation results support this hypothesis showing that as hours of video gaming increased, GPA decreased, ρ(18) = −.58, $p$ = .007.

</td></tr>
</table>

## 7.2 Mann–Whitney *U* Test as a Test of Differences between Two Means

When you want to test if there is a significant difference between two samples, but the data that you have collected do not meet the general assumptions of the independent-samples *t* test covered in Chapter 4, Section 1 (e.g., the variables are not normally distributed or the variables are ordinal), then the Mann–Whitney *U* test is a good choice to test your hypothesis. Mann–Whitney *U* allows you to test differences between two samples on an ordinal variable or a variable that is not normally distributed.

**THE DATA**

For this Mann–Whitney *U* test, we will use data from an experiment conducted by some of my research methods students. The students wanted to test the impact of music with or without words on self-reported student learning. Twenty students were randomly assigned to listen to a song while reading a chapter in their *Introduction to Psychology* textbook. Students were assigned to listen to either a song with words or the same song without words (just instrumental). After students completed reading the chapter, the students self-reported how much they believed they comprehended from their reading on a 5-point ordinal scale, from 1(*not at all*) to 5 (*completely*).

We entered two columns of data. The first column was the group to which the participants were assigned, called *musictype*, either the music without words (coded as a 1) or music with words (coded as a 2). The second column was their self-reported comprehension from 1 to 5, called *comprehension*. We made sure to define the *Measure* of the dependent variable as *Scale* in *Variable View* when setting up the data for entry, because the analysis would not run without a scale-specified *Measure* for the dependent variable.

Here are what the data look like in *Data View*:

The researchers hypothesized that the group that listened to music without words would self-report higher comprehension on the 5-point comprehension scale than the group that listened to music with words. To test this hypothesis, a nonparametric test is needed because comprehension is an ordinal variable and not quantitative data. Here is how to run the Mann–Whitney *U* to test the hypothesis that there is a significant difference in comprehension for the two groups—those who listened to music with words and those who listened to music without words.

Select from the Top Menu Bar:

ANALYZE → NONPARAMETRIC → INDEPENDENT SAMPLES

*SPSS Commands* **7.2**

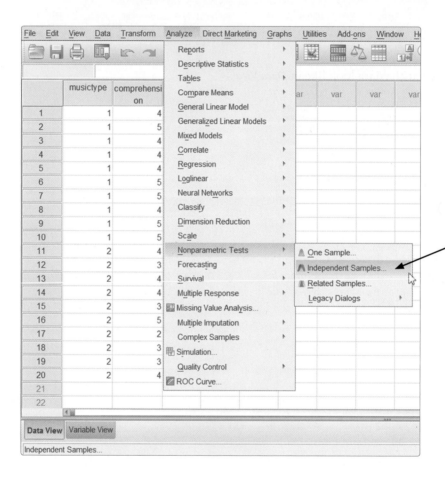

In the *Nonparametric Tests: Two or More Independent Samples Objective* pop-up window, select *Automatically compare distributions across groups*, then select the *Fields* tab.

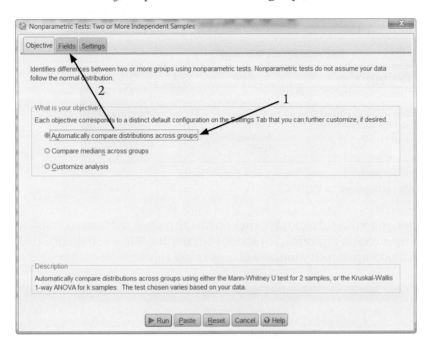

In the *Fields* pop-up window, highlight *comprehension* and click the arrow pointing to the *Test Fields* box, and highlight *musictype* and click the arrow pointing to the *Groups* box, then click ▶ *Run*. Again, it is important to note that SPSS only allows you to use variables that are listed as *Scale* in *Test Fields* box, so you must define your dependent variable as *Scale* in *Variable View* of your data entry.

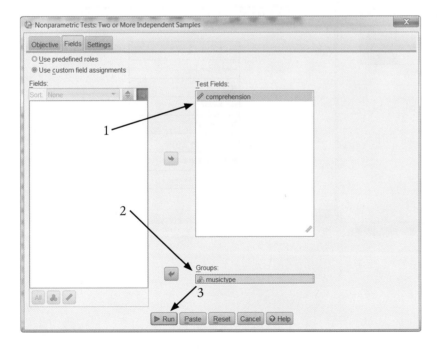

When you run this analysis, SPSS gives you the following nonparametric Mann–Whitney *U* output.

**Nonparametric Tests**

**Hypothesis Test Summary**

| | Null Hypothesis | Test | Sig. | Decision |
|---|---|---|---|---|
| 1 | The distribution of comprehension is the same across categories of musictype. | Independent-Samples Mann-Whitney U Test | .011[1] | Reject the null hypothesis. |

Asymptotic significances are displayed. The significance level is .05.

[1]Exact significance is displayed for this test.

For this output, you will need to double-click on this *Hypothesis Test Summary* table to obtain all of the necessary information about your results. When you double-click on this table, a pop-up output window will appear like this:

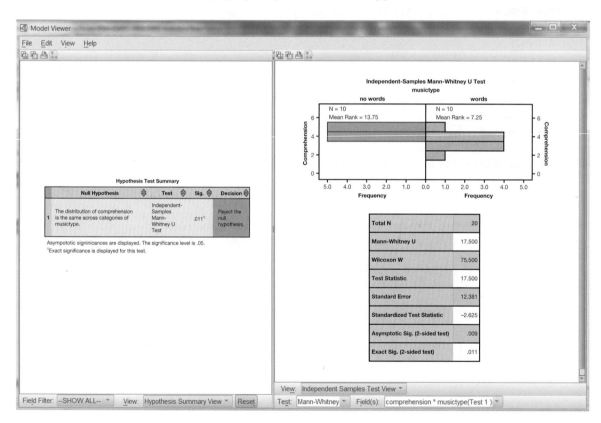

You will need the information on the right-hand side of this *Modal Viewer* pop-up window:

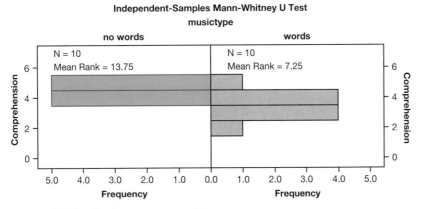

### Independent-Samples Mann-Whitney U Test

| Total N | 20 |
|---|---|
| Mann-Whitney U | 17.500 |
| Wilcoxon W | 72.500 |
| Test Statistic | 17.500 |
| Standard Error | 12.381 |
| Standardized Test Statistic | −2.625 |
| Asymptotic Sig. (2-sided test) | .009 |
| Exact Sig. (2-sided test) | .011 |

*Interpretation* 7.2

Much like an independent-samples *t* test, the Mann–Whitney *U* tests differences in self-reported comprehension for the group that listened to music with words compared to the group that listened to music without words. According to the Mann–Whitney *U* test, there is a significant difference based on the *p* value (*Sig.*) of .011. The group that listened to the music with words ($M_{rank}$ = 7.25) reported comprehending less than the group that listened to the music without words ($M_{rank}$ = 13.75).

For the Mann–Whitney $U$ test, we will need the Mean Ranks, the Mann–Whitney $U$ statistic, the $z$ score (found under *Standardized Test Statistic*), and the $p$ value. In addition, we will need to calculate a measure of effect size called $r$. This is a statistic that needs to be hand-calculated using the following formula:

$$r = \frac{z}{\sqrt{N}}$$

For this problem, the calculations for $r$ are:

$$r = \frac{-2.625}{\sqrt{20}} = .59$$

So, your APA-style Results paragraph should look like this:

> We hypothesized that the group that listened to music with words would report significantly lower comprehension than the group that listened to music without words. As hypothesized, the group that listened to music with words ($M_{rank} = 7.25$) reported comprehending significantly less than the group that listened to the music without words ($M_{rank} = 13.75$), $U = 17.5$, $z = -2.63$, $p = .011$, $r = .59$.

# 7.3 Kruskal–Wallis Test as a Test of Between-Group Differences

When you want to test if there is a significant difference between two or more samples, but the data that you collected do not meet the general assumptions of the one-way ANOVA covered in Chapter 4, Section 2 (e.g., the variables are not normally distributed or the variables are ordinal), then the Kruskal–Wallis test is a good choice to test your hypothesis. Kruskal–Wallis allows you to test differences between two or more samples on an ordinal variable or a variable that is not normally distributed.

**THE DATA**

For this Kruskal–Wallis test, we will build on data from the previous experiment in Chapter 7, Section 2. In this experiment, the researchers wanted to test the impact of music with or without words on self-reported student learning. We will add one more level of the independent variable of *musictype* by adding ten more participants who did the same study with no music at all. In this expanded study, students were randomly assigned to one of three groups—music with words, music without words (just instrumental), or no music at all—and tasked with reading a chapter in their *Introduction to Psychology* textbook. After they completed reading the chapter, the students self-reported how much they believed they comprehended from their reading on a 5-point ordinal scale from 1(*not at all*) to 5 (*completely*).

We entered two columns of data. The first column was the group to which the participants were assigned, called *musictype*—music without words was coded as 1, music with words was coded as 2, and no music at all was coded as 3. The second column was their self-reported comprehension from 1 to 5, called *comprehension*. We made sure to define the *Measure* of our dependent variable as *Scale* in *Variable View* when setting up the data for entry, because the analysis would not run without a scale-specified *Measure* for the dependent variable.

Here are what the data look like in *Data View*:

The researchers hypothesized that the group that had no music at all would self-report the highest comprehension of the three music groups on the 5-point comprehension scale. To test this hypothesis, a nonparametric test is needed because comprehension is an ordinal variable and not quantitative data. Here is how to run the Kruskal–Wallis test to test the hypothesis that comprehension is significantly different among the three music groups.

*SPSS Commands 7.3*

Select from the Top Menu Bar:

ANALYZE → NONPARAMETRIC TESTS → INDEPENDENT SAMPLES

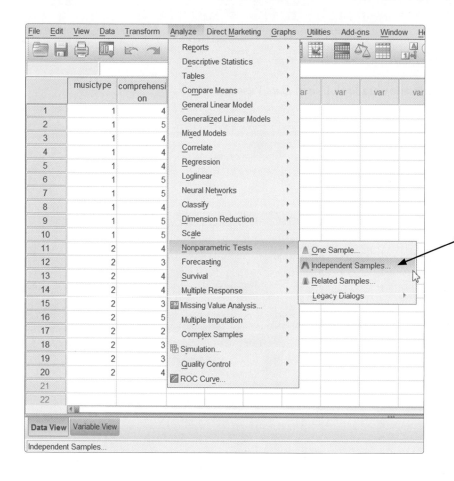

In the *Nonparametric Tests: Two or More Independent Samples Objective* pop-up window, select *Automatically compare distributions across groups*, then select the *Fields* tab.

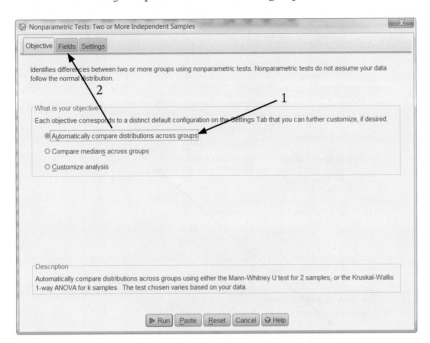

In the *Fields* pop-up window, highlight *comprehension* and click the arrow pointing to the *Test Fields* box, and highlight *musictype* and click the arrow pointing to the *Groups* box, then click the *Settings* tab.

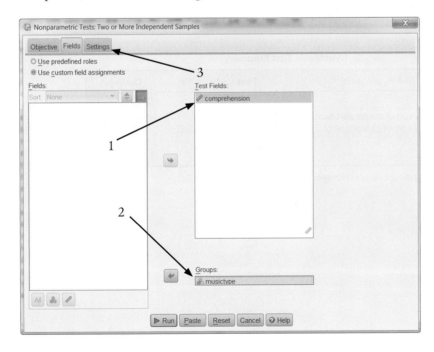

In the *Settings* pop-up window, select *Customize tests* and then check *Kruskal–Wallis 1-way ANOVA*, then choose *All pairwise* from the *Multiple comparisons* drop-down. Finally, click ▶ *Run*.

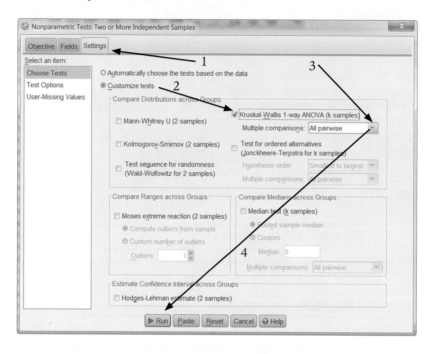

When you run this analysis, SPSS gives you the following nonparametric Kruskal–Wallis output.

**Nonparametric Tests**

**Hypothesis Test Summary**

| | Null Hypothesis | Test | Sig. | Decision |
|---|---|---|---|---|
| 1 | The distribution of comprehension is the same across categories of musictype. | Independent-Samples Kruskal-Wallis Tst | .007 | Reject the null hypothesis. |

Asymptotic significances are displayed. The significance level is .05.

For this output, you will need to double-click on this Hypothesis Test Summary table to obtain all of the necessary information about your results. When you double-click on this table, a pop-up output window will appear like this:

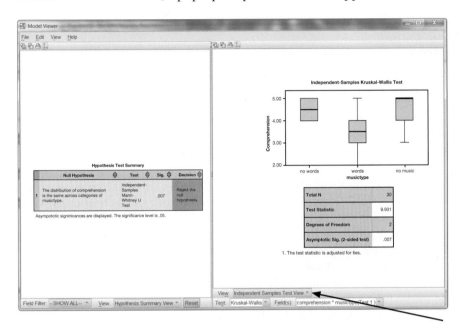

You will also need to select *Pairwise Comparisons* under *View* to see which levels of the independent variable are significantly different from each other.

**Pairwise Comparisons of musictype**

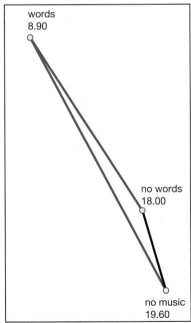

Each node shows the sample average rank of musictype.

| Sample1-Sample2 | Test Statistic | Std. Error | Std. Test Statistic | Sig. | Adj.Sig. |
|---|---|---|---|---|---|
| words-no words | 9.100 | 3.663 | 2.484 | .013 | .039 |
| words-no music | −10.700 | 3.663 | −2.921 | .003 | .010 |
| no words-no music | −1.600 | 3.663 | −.437 | .662 | 1.000 |

Each row tests the null hypothesis that the Sample 1 and Sample 2 distributions are the same.

Asymptotic significances (2-sided tests) are displayed. The significance level is .05.

*Interpretation 7.3*

Much like ANOVA, the Kruskal–Wallis tests differences in self-reported comprehension among the three groups: no music, music without words, and music with words. Overall, music condition significantly affects self-reported comprehension because the $p$ value for the Kruskal–Wallis statistic is less than .05 ($p = .007$). When assessing the pairwise comparisons, we can see that the groups exposed to no music ($M_{rank} = 19.60$) and music without words ($M_{rank} = 18.00$) were not significantly different from each other ($p = .66$), but both were significantly higher on comprehension than the music with words group ($M_{rank} = 8.90$). This shows that not all music is detrimental to comprehension, just music with words.

*APA Style 7.3*

For the Kruskal–Wallis test, we will need the Mean Ranks, the Kruskal–Wallis statistic (noted as $H$ in APA style), the degrees of freedom, and the $p$ value. In addition, we will need the $p$ values for the pairwise comparisons. This is what your APA-style Results section would look like for this finding:

We hypothesized that self-reported comprehension would be lowest when participants listened to music with words compared to participants who listened to music without words or participants who did not listen to music at all. Comprehension was significantly affected by exposure to music overall, $H(2) = 9.93$, $p = .007$. Pairwise comparisons with adjusted $p$ values showed that the difference between the no-music group ($M_{rank} = 19.60$) and the music without words group ($M_{rank} = 18.00$), $p = .66$, was not significant. However, as hypothesized, there were significant differences between the music with words group ($M_{rank} = 8.90$) and the no-music group ($p = .010$), as well as the music with words group and the music without words group ($p = .039$). This shows that not all music is detrimental to comprehension, just music with words.

# 7.4 Wilcoxon Signed-Ranks Test as a Test of Within-Group Differences

When you want to test if there is a significant difference in levels of an independent variable and the same participants receive both levels (within-groups), but the data that you have collected do not meet the general assumptions of the paired-samples *t* test covered in Chapter 4, Section 3 (e.g., the variables are not normally distributed or the variables are ordinal), then the Wilcoxon Signed-Ranks test is a good choice to test your hypothesis. Wilcoxon Signed-Ranks allows you to test differences between two levels of an independent variable that is measured using an ordinal variable or a variable that is not normally distributed.

---

### THE DATA

For this Wilcoxon Signed-Ranks test, we will use data that were collected from students at the beginning and again at the end of the semester about opinions regarding group projects. The dependent variable was a Likert-scale question about agreement with the following statement:

**Working in groups is the best way to accomplish doing research.**

Strongly Disagree    Disagree    Neither Disagree nor Agree    Agree    Strongly Agree

We wanted to test if attitudes toward working in groups changes significantly from the beginning to the end of the semester after students have had an opportunity to conduct a research study in a group. The same students answer this exact question both on the first and last day of class.

---

The dependent variable is the Likert-scale opinion question about working in groups. This variable is called *WorkGroup1* for the data from the first day of class, and *WorkGroup2* for the data from the last day of class. The values are from 1 (*Strongly Disagree*) to 5 (*Strongly Agree*). We made sure to define the *Measure* of our dependent variable (in this example, both *WorkGroup1* and *WorkGroup2*) as *Scale* in *Variable View* when setting up the data for entry, because the analysis would not run without a scale-specified *Measure* for the dependent variable.

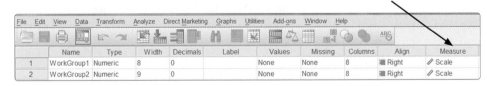

Here are what your data look like in *Data View*:

| | WorkGroup1 | WorkGroup2 |
|---|---|---|
| 1 | 4 | 4 |
| 2 | 4 | 5 |
| 3 | 3 | 3 |
| 4 | 5 | 2 |
| 5 | 4 | 1 |
| 6 | 2 | 1 |
| 7 | 4 | 4 |
| 8 | 4 | 4 |
| 9 | 5 | 1 |
| 10 | 3 | 1 |
| 11 | 4 | 4 |
| 12 | 5 | 3 |
| 13 | 2 | 2 |
| 14 | 4 | 4 |
| 15 | 5 | 3 |
| 16 | 4 | 2 |
| 17 | 4 | 2 |
| 18 | 4 | 2 |
| 19 | 5 | 4 |
| 20 | 3 | 3 |
| 21 | 1 | 1 |
| 22 | 4 | 5 |
| 23 | 1 | 1 |

The researchers hypothesized that opinions about group projects would be more negative on the last day of class than on the first day. To test this hypothesis, a nonparametric test is needed because the dependent variable is an ordinal variable and not quantitative data. Here is how to run the *Wilcoxon signed-rank test* to test the hypothesis that opinion about working in groups is significantly different at the end of the semester than at the beginning.

*SPSS Commands 7.4*

Select from the Top Menu Bar:

ANALYZE → NONPARAMETRIC TESTS → RELATED SAMPLES

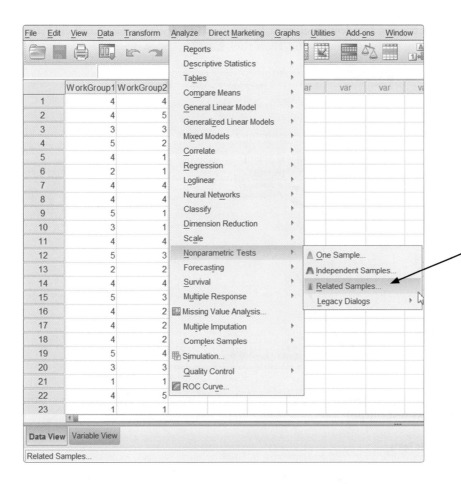

In the *Nonparametric Tests: Two or More Related Samples Objective* pop-up window, select *Automatically compare observed data to hypothesized*, then select the *Fields* tab.

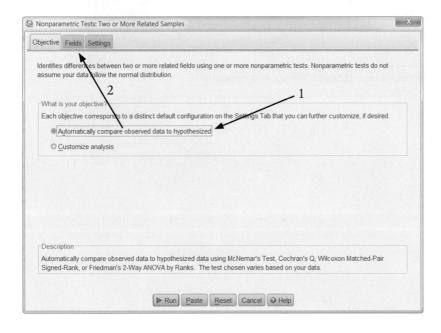

In the *Fields* pop-up window, highlight *WorkGroup1* and *WorkGroup2* and click the arrow pointing to the *Test Fields* box, then click ▶ *Run*.

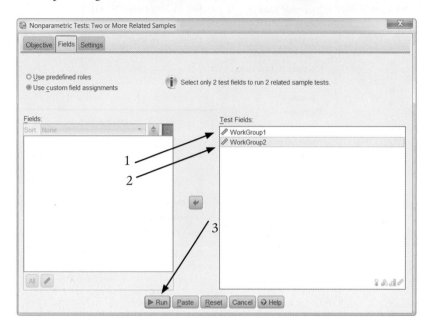

When you run this analysis, SPSS gives you the following nonparametric Wilcoxon Signed-Ranks test output:

**Nonparametric Tests**

**Hypothesis Test Summary**

| | Null Hypothesis | Test | Sig. | Decision |
|---|---|---|---|---|
| 1 | The median of differences between WorkGroup1 and WorkGroup2 equals 0. | Related-Samples Wilcoxon Signed Rank Test | .000 | Reject the null hypothesis. |

Asymptotic significances are displayed. The significance level is .05.

For this output, you will need to double-click on this Hypothesis Test Summary table to obtain all of the necessary information about your results. When you double-click on this table, a pop-up output window will appear like this:

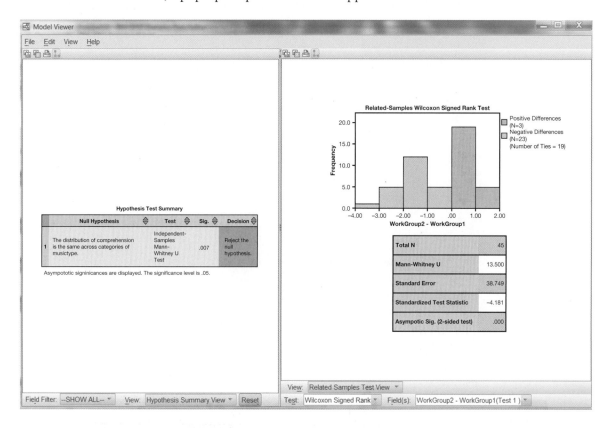

Much like a paired-samples *t* test, the Wilcoxon Signed-Rank test can test differences in the Likert-scale opinion question about group projects. Data is collected at two times: at the beginning and end of the semester. The same students provided both ratings. According to the Wilcoxon Signed-Rank test, there is a significant difference because the *p* value (*Sig.*) is less than .05 (here, because the *p* value listed is .000, we will report it as $p < .001$). Because the standardized test statistic (*z* score) is negative ($z = -4.18$), we know that opinion becomes more negative at the end of the semester compared to the beginning of the semester. In addition, in the graph you can see that there were far more negative differences (23) between first and last day of class opinions as opposed to ties (19) or positive differences (3), which also shows that opinions became more negative overall.

*Interpretation*
**7.4**

For the Wilcoxon Signed-Rank test, we will need the Wilcoxon Signed-Rank statistic (noted as *T* in APA style), the *z* score (found under *Standardized Test Statistic*), and the *p* value. In addition, we will need to calculate a measure of effect size called *r*. This is a statistic that needs to be hand-calculated using the following formula:

$$r = \frac{z}{\sqrt{N}}$$

For this problem, the calculations for *r* are:

$$r = \frac{-4.181}{\sqrt{45}} = .62$$

So, your APA-style Results paragraph should look like this:

> We hypothesized that responses to a Likert-scale opinion question about working in groups would be significantly lower on the last day of class compared to the first day. As hypothesized, students held significantly lower opinions of group work at the end of the semester compared to the beginning, $T = 13.50$, $z = -4.18$, $p < .001$, $r = .62$.

# Photo Credits

Courtesy of International Business Machines Corporation, © International Business Machines Corporation. "SPSS Inc." was acquired by IBM in October, 2009. "IBM SPSS Statistics software ("SPSS"). IBM, the IBM logo, ibm.com, and SPSS are trademarks or registered trademarks of International Business Machines Corporation, registered in many jurisdictions worldwide. Other product and service names might be trademarks of IBM or other companies. A current list of IBM trademarks is available on the Web at "IBM Copyright and trademark information" at www. ibm.com/legal/copytrade.shtml.

## Chapter 1

**(All):** Reprint Courtesy of International Business Machines Corporation, © International Business Machines Corporation. **(page 14):** Courtesy of Qualtrics.

## Chapter 2

**(All):** Reprint Courtesy of International Business Machines Corporation, © International Business Machines Corporation.

## Chapter 3

**(All):** Reprint Courtesy of International Business Machines Corporation, © International Business Machines Corporation.

## Chapter 4

**Figures 4.1 (left), 4.2 (left), 4.8, and 4.16 (left) (casual woman):** BEW Authors/ Agefotostock; **Figures 4.1 (right), 4.2 (right), and 4.16 (right) (professional woman):** Juice Images; **(balance, all):** Reprint Courtesy of International Business Machines Corporation, © International Business Machines Corporation.

## Chapter 5

**Figures 5.1, 5.2, and 5.17 (left) (casual woman):** BEW Authors/Agefotostock; **Figure 5.17 (second from left) (professional woman):** Juice Images/Agefotostock; **Figure 5.17 (second from right) (professional man):** Shutterstock; **Figure 5.17 (right) (casual man):** Gallery Stock; **(balance, all):** Reprint Courtesy of International Business Machines Corporation, © International Business Machines Corporation.

## Chapter 6

**(All):** Reprint Courtesy of International Business Machines Corporation, © International Business Machines Corporation.

## Chapter 7

**(All):** Reprint Courtesy of International Business Machines Corporation, © International Business Machines Corporation.

# Index